T0106518

'ZONIES'

Recipes for a Healthy Life

Don't Weight.......Get Cooking!

40% Carbohydrates, 30% Proteins and 30% Favorable Fats

Chef Phil Andriano

Order this book online at www.trafford.com
or email orders@trafford.com

Most Trafford titles are also available at major online book retailers.

Printed in the United States of America.

ISBN: 978-1-4907-2589-5 (sc)
ISBN: 978-1-4907-2588-8 (e)

Library of Congress Control Number: 2014901721

Trafford rev. 01/27/2014

 www.trafford.com

North America & international
toll-free: 1 888 232 4444 (USA & Canada)
fax: 812 355 4082

To Michael S. and to all those who dared make a lifestyle change, followed a balanced diet, and realized their goal of gaining health and losing weight.

Contents

Foreword

As corporate executive chef for Chefs Diet™, Philip Andriano created meals that taste great and are based on Nobel Prize-winning science popularized by the Dr. Sears's Zone Diet, balancing a ratio of 40 percent carbohydrates, 30 percent protein, and 30 percent favorable fat. His culinary prowess, creativity, and understanding of dieters' needs are apparent in every dish, resulting in menus that are as diverse as they are enjoyable. Leading a team of fifteen trained chefs, Chef Andriano flawlessly translated such indulgences as *Eggs Benedict, Chicken Cacciatore with Red Pepper Polenta,* and *Double Chocolate Chip Cookies* into waistline-friendly dishes.

From the start Philip's meals have been reviewed by multiple national publications, including *Health Magazine, Time Magazine,* and the Associated Press. As corporate executive chef for Chefs Diet, Philip's meals have been seen on numerous television programs, such as Entertainment Tonight, CNBC's "Closing Bell," and several shows on the Style Network.

As former champion of the New York State Seafood Challenge and bronze medalist of the Nationwide Seafood Challenge, Chef Andriano has more than demonstrated his ability to embrace and successfully meet a challenge. And for a chef, there are a few things more challenging than creating food that is exceptional in taste *and* diet-friendly. Not surprisingly, Chef Andriano has accomplished just that at Chefs Diet™.

Preface

The Michael S. Story

It was some time ago that I met Michael; I guess you can say I knew him before and after. Each day on my way to work, I would pass by his butcher shop. It had a large plate glass window, and Michael could be seen bending over the butcher block wincing in discomfort.

Michael was at least 375 lbs. in total misery and poor health; the man I thought was in need of help and a friend, so I stopped in to talk. I explained what a balanced diet could do for him, and I set a plan in motion for him to follow. From there on out, as we discussed the diet and he became more educated, his attitude began to change along with his health. I watched the pounds fall off and watched him become thinner and fit. His energy returned to him, enabling him to do things that he thought he would never do again, in short he rejuvenated his life. I'm very proud of Michael, his goal was to lose weight and he did, 150 lbs. in one year, just amazing! He stuck to it and now has a new ongoing quest to remain healthy and fit for the rest of his life. This is a real success story and with guidance you too can reach the goals to achieve optimum health, remember, sometimes we all can use a friend.

Sincerely,
Chef Phil Andriano

Testimonial
By
Michael S.

My name is Michael; I am fifty years old and have had a weight problem my entire life. I would lose weight only to put it back on and end up heavier than before.

I tried a variety of diets, all of them worked to varying degrees, but none of them was a solution; that is until I discovered the 'Zone', when I started the diet I was over 370 lbs.

That's when I met Chef Phil Andriano, the original chef of the 'Zone' meal plan. With his guidance I lost 150 lbs. in one year and over 185 lbs. in a year and a half. I lost all of this weight without being hungry and eating a nice variety of foods. The best thing about the diet was I finally learned how to eat. It's been 6 months since I hit my target weight and I haven't gained back a pound, because I've learned that it's not how many calories you eat but how and when you eat them. This diet has changed my life and it can change yours too.

Yours Truly,
Michael S.

Acknowledgment

For over a decade, I have devoted my culinary career to the cause of obesity and a cure to its end. As I worked toward this goal, I realized the way to a healthy lifestyle started with the foods we consume; as they say "you are what you eat" has always proven to be true. Consuming unhealthy foods can begin with our youth, and unfortunately, the bad habit can stay with us throughout our adult lives. Not eating properly denies us the nutrition necessary for a healthy lifestyle and immunity toward many diseases, such as child and adult diabetes.

The title of this book, "Zonies," is attributed to those individuals who put their health foremost and began the quest for a better life. I categorize a grouping of people under the Zonies heading because they understand the importance of a nutritionally balanced diet and know the necessity of maintaining it on a daily basis.

They are of an elite class who are in the know, daring to go beyond convention, directing their lives toward a goal, and therefore, benefiting accordingly.

So how about you? Dare to come along and get in the know. It's not only the wise thing to do; it's the right thing to do!

Notice: Please be advised that this diet program and recipes herein do not represent a professionally sanctioned medical diet. Results may vary. Please consult your physician's advice before beginning any diet program.

Introduction

I want to congratulate you all on your decision to begin a healthy lifestyle through a balanced diet. In the next two weeks, you will begin a culinary journey that will give you an understanding of how easy it is to balance, portion control, bake, and cook healthy and delicious meals.

Do you realize how amazing our bodies are? It is incredible how it turns what we eat into energy so we may do what is necessary to carry on through life. By eating a balanced diet, we benefit from the right nutrients found in each food source. When we make the right choice in our diet, we put ourselves on the ultimate track to a healthy lifestyle.

As an expert in the Zone Diet and chef to some of today's most popular celebrities and countless many others who have benefited from this diet, I can offer you a *tool* to begin a 40/30/30 balanced ratio of favorable carbohydrates, proteins, and fats. With this book, you can begin preparing the same gourmet meals celebrities are eating, and in your own home.

Knowing how difficult it is to lose weight while dieting, limiting yourself to strict healthy eating habits can lead you away from many enjoyable food experiences. If this means giving up the foods you love most, then dieting becomes more of a hindrance than a help. You can still enjoy eating by learning how to make better and healthier choices; the key to good health is not to overindulge, but to balance and eat in moderation.

In this book, you will receive weekly menus complete with shopping list and recipes that are calorically evaluated, educating you with each experience.

Each day includes: Breakfast, Lunch, Snack, Dinner, and Dessert; all with easy to follow recipes and methods. The total caloric content is calculated for each day and does not exceed 1,700 calories, staying well within the Zone limits. Remember meals should be eaten in succession to receive ultimate nutritional value without over indulging in calorie intake; this makes for a well-balanced diet.

These recipes are designed to help educate those in need of dieting and achieving a healthy lifestyle; it gives the reader an easy recipe for success by showing you how to prepare these sensible yet decadent meals.

There are many baking or cookbooks on the market, but none directs the reader toward the usage of more nutritious ingredients; these recipes are unique, because it gives the 40/30/30 ratio balance of macronutrients. It shows the caloric evaluation between carbohydrates, proteins, and favorable fats, giving the reader an understanding where calories are derived.

It is designed not to be technical; recipes and methods are easily followed with the layman in mind. Once again, it is for those who are looking to find an alternative so they may remain true to their diet and begin a healthy lifestyle.

I am sure there are many of you who are new to a balanced diet program, yet I know you will be pleasantly surprised when you begin making these delicious and easy to prepare meals. I believe all those who find it hard work to follow a diet plan and don't want to give up their favorite foods doing so will enjoy the benefits of these recipes.

Get Cooking! Get Healthy!

MENU
Days 1-7

	Monday	Tuesday	Wednesday	Thursday	Friday	Saturday	Sunday
	Day 1	Day 2	Day 3	Day 4	Day 5	Day 6	Day 7
Breakfast	Cottage Cheese Blintzes w/ Fruit Sauce & Assorted Melon Cup	Mexican Egg Muffin w/ Festive Salsa Fresco	Sweet Potato Pancakes w/ Scrambled Egg Substitute Maple Syrup	Hawaiian Country Breakfast Cereal w/ Banana	Pumpernickel "Mini Bagel" w/ Smoked Nova Salmon Red Onion, Capers	Scrambled Eggs on English Muffin w/ Black Forest Ham & Sautéed Spinach, Sauce Choron	Orange Cranberry Power Muffin w/ Orange Soy Butter
Lunch	Shrimp Salad w/ Berry Vinaigrette	Turkey Salad Platter w/ Seedless Grapes & Yogurt Dill Dressing	Grilled Portobello Napoleon	Grilled Veggie Quesadilla	Catalina Chicken Salad w/ Mango & Cran Raisins Red Delicious Apple	Crab Salad w/ Melon & Herbed Mayonnaise	Monterey Steak Salad Platter w/ Chili Roasted Corn Cob
Snack	Stuffed Cabbage Rolls w/ Sweet & Sour Sauce	Brushetta w/ Roasted Garlic Puree & Melted Mozzarella	Fresh Ahi Tuna & Garlic Aioli On Tortilla Chips	Spaghetti Squash w/ Mozzarella Tomatoes Basil Vinaigrette	Wilted Spinach & Hearty Cheese Dip	Toasted Chevre Cheese w/ Table Grapes	Black Strap BBQ Shrimp w/ Georgia Peach Compote
Dinner	Cajun Chicken Breast w/ Collard Greens & Cornbread	Veal Cacciatore w/ Red Pepper Polenta	Beef Bracciola w/ Roasted Tomato Sauce & Whole Grain linguini	Port au Prince' Maple Marinated Grilled Pork Loin w/ Pecan Rice	Roasted Lamb Top Round w/ Garlicky Potatoes & Broccoli Rape	Stuffed Bell Peppers w/ Garbanzo Beans & Sun Dried Tomatoes Salad	Cheese & Red Pepper Roasted Chicken Breast on Fennel

Dessert	White Chocolate Cheesecake Bars w/ Chocolate Crust	Ginger Carrot Cake	White & Dark Chocolate Chip Cookie	Almond Fruit Bars	Pumpkin Cheese Cake Bars	Butterscotch Chip Cookies	Espresso Cupcakes
Daily Calories	1,418.80	1,314.80	1,447.00	1,668.30	1,428.60	1,422.60	1,528.30

Day 1

Breakfast

Cottage Cheese Blintzes with Fruit Sauce and Assorted Melon Cup

Yield: 1 Serving

30% Protein:	6oz. or 2/3 cp. Nonfat Cottage Cheese	
40% Carbohydrate:	2 ea. Crepe Shells	
	½ cp. Assorted Berries	
	1 tb. Lemon Juice	
	1 tsp. Sugar	
	6 oz. or 2/3 cp. Assorted Melon (Diced)	
	or ½ Melon	
30% Fat:	2 tb. Low-fat Cream Cheese	

Method:
1) Mix or blend the cream cheese with the cottage cheese and divide mixture between crepes.
2) Spoon in mixture evenly and fold over blintz style (pocket fold).
3) In a sauce pot over low heat cook the sugar, lemon juice, and berries until a glaze is formed. Let cool.

Serving:
1) Place blintzes on a plate and top with the sauce, surround with the fresh melon.

Breakfast Alternate: Ricotta Cheese Blintzes with Raspberry Sauce
1) Omit the cottage cheese and replace with skim ricotta.

Nutrition Facts	
1 Serving	
Amount Per Serving	
Calories	376.0
Total Fat	5.0 g
Saturated Fat	2.3 g
Polyunsaturated Fat	0.9 g
Monounsaturated Fat	1.4 g
Cholesterol	64.6 mg
Sodium	1,149.1 mg
Potassium	522.7 mg
Total Carbohydrate	45.7 g
Dietary Fiber	2.6 g
Sugars	26.6 g
Protein	42.4 g
Vitamin	A 38.7 %
Vitamin B-12	26.0 %
Vitamin B-6	16.8 %
Vitamin C	85.9 %
Vitamin D	0.0 %
Vitamin E	4.1 %
Calcium	31.4 %
Copper	6.3 %
Folate	15.5 %
Iron	5.2 %
Magnesium	7.2 %
Manganese	10.3 %
Niacin	5.9 %
Pantothenic Acid	6.3 %
Phosphorus	32.3 %
Riboflavin	20.1 %
Selenium	29.2 %
Thiamin	9.5 %
Zinc	8.2 %

Day 1

Lunch

Shrimp Salad with Berry Vinaigrette

Yield: 1 Serving

30% Protein: 6 ea. / 6 oz. Shrimp (16/20's per lb.)

40% Carbohydrate: 2 cps. Mesclun Salad Greens
                     ¼ cp. Fresh Blackberries
                     ¼ cp. Fresh Strawberries
                     5 ea. Spears Asparagus
                     1 tsp. Honey
                     2 oz. or ¼ cp. Raspberry Vinegar

30% Fat: 2 tsp. Canola Oil

Method:
1) Combine the oil, vinegar, and honey to make vinaigrette, reserve.
2) Peel and devein the shrimp, then poach in simmering water until done and opaque in color. Cool and reserve.
3) Cook the asparagus in simmering water until tender. Cool and reserve.

Serving:
1) Place the greens in a bowl and surround with fresh berries and asparagus, top with the shrimp.
2) Pour the vinaigrette over, coating the salad.

Lunch Alternate: Egg Salad with Berry Vinaigrette
1) Omit the shrimp and replace with 2 ea. sliced hard-boiled eggs.

Nutrition Facts	
1 Serving	
Amount Per Serving	
Calories	336.4
Total Fat	11.2 g
Saturated Fat	1.2 g
Polyunsaturated Fat	3.6 g
Monounsaturated Fat	5.7 g
Cholesterol	331.5 mg
Sodium	393.3 mg
Potassium	670.5 mg
Total Carbohydrate	22.3 g
Dietary Fiber	5.1 g
Sugars	13.3 g
Protein	38.4 g
Vitamin A	75.8 %
Vitamin B-12	42.2 %
Vitamin B-6	17.0 %
Vitamin C	88.0 %
Vitamin D	0.0 %
Vitamin E	21.2 %
Calcium	12.0 %
Copper	26.5 %
Folate	25.7 %
Iron	40.2 %
Magnesium	23.2 %
Manganese	47.0 %
Niacin	26.7 %
Pantothenic Acid	9.0 %
Phosphorus	28.7 %
Riboflavin	10.2 %
Selenium	99.0 %
Thiamin	10.3 %
Zinc	20.6 %

Day 1

Snack

Stuffed Cabbage Rolls with Sweet and Sour Sauce

Yield: 1 Serving

30% Protein:	2 oz. Ground 93% Lean Beef
	½ oz. Liquid Egg Substitute or Liquid Egg Whites

40% Carbohydrate:	¼ cp. Cooked Brown Rice
	2 ea. Napa/Chinese Cabbage Leaves
	¼ tsp. Cinnamon Powder
	½ cp. Prepared Tomato Sauce
	½ tsp. Brown Sugar
	1 tb. Minced Sp. Onion
	1 oz. Cider Vinegar

30% Fat:	1 tsp. Canola Oil

Method:
Suggestion: Prepare the cabbage rolls in advance, steps 1-3 reserve refrigerated, then braise steps 4-5, and serve heated.

1) In the oil sauté the onions and beef. Let cool then add the rice and egg.
2) Blanch the cabbage leaves by simmering in water until cooked and tender. Cool and reserve.
3) Double up the leaves and place the meat mixture in the middle and roll.
4) Combine the tomato sauce with the vinegar and sugar.
5) Place the cabbage rolls in a bake-able dish, pour the sauce over, and braise the cabbage at 350 degrees for twenty minutes or until the meat is cooked.

Serving:
1) Place on a plate and top with the sauce.

Snack Alternate: Turkey-Stuffed Cabbage Rolls with Sweet and Sour Sauce
1) Omit the beef and replace with 2 oz. ground turkey.

Nutrition Facts	
1 Serving	
Amount Per Serving	
Calories	184.4
Total Fat	6.8 g
Saturated Fat	1.8 g
Polyunsaturated Fat	0.8 g
Monounsaturated Fat	1.4 g
Cholesterol	32.7 mg
Sodium	391.1 mg
Potassium	396.1 mg
Total Carbohydrate	17.1 g
Dietary Fiber	2.5 g
Sugars	6.6 g
Protein	15.4 g
Vitamin A	8.8 %
Vitamin B-12	5.0 %
Vitamin B-6	6.1 %
Vitamin C	24.6 %
Vitamin D	2.5 %
Vitamin E	7.8 %
Calcium	3.8 %
Copper	5.1 %
Folate	8.9 %
Iron	8.5 %
Magnesium	5.9 %
Manganese	14.8 %
Niacin	3.6 %
Pantothenic Acid	4.9 %
Phosphorus	4.8 %
Riboflavin	15.8 %
Selenium	6.3 %
Thiamin	4.8 %
Zinc	2.4 %

Day 2

Snack

Brushetta with Roasted Garlic Puree and Melted Mozzarella

Yield: 1 Serving

30% Protein:	2 oz. or 4 tb. Shredded Skim Mozzarella
40% Carbohydrate:	2 ea. Thin Slice French bread (1/4") Toasted 2 ea. Garlic Cloves (Roasted)
30% Fat:	½ tsp. Olive oil

Method:
1) Roast garlic in 250 degree oven until golden brown, cool, and reserve.
2) Spread the oil evenly over each slice of bread and top with a spread of roasted garlic puree.
3) Top each bread slice with 1 oz. Mozzarella and bake until cheese melts.

Serving: Place on a plate and eat heated.

Snack Alternate: Skim Mozzarella and Whole Fresh Pear

Nutrition Facts	
1 Serving	
Amount Per Serving	
Calories	202.1
Total Fat	9.0 g
Saturated Fat	4.6 g
Polyunsaturated Fat	0.4 g
Monounsaturated Fat	3.6 g
Cholesterol	24.7 mg
Sodium	198.6 mg
Potassium	46.9 mg
Total Carbohydrate	2.1 g
Dietary Fiber	0.1 g
Sugars	0.0 g
Protein	10.5 g
Vitamin A	5.0 %
Vitamin B-12	5.8 %
Vitamin B-6	3.2 %
Vitamin C	1.5 %
Vitamin D	0.0 %
Vitamin E	2.3 %
Calcium	28.0 %
Copper	1.0 %
Folate	1.0 %
Iron	0.8 %
Magnesium	2.6 %
Manganese	2.6 %
Niacin	0.3 %
Pantothenic Acid	0.5 %
Phosphorus	20.1 %
Riboflavin	7.8 %
Selenium	9.3 %
Thiamin	0.9 %
Zinc	8.1 %

Day 2

Dinner

Veal Cacciatore with Red Pepper Polenta

Yield: 1 Serving

30% Protein:	4 oz. Veal Scaloppini or Stew Meat
	1 tbs. Parmesan Cheese

40% Carbohydrate:	¼ cp. Dry Polenta Mix
	1 tbs. Red Pepper (minced)
	1 tbs. Onion (minced)
	¼ cp. Button Mushrooms
	¼ cp. Green Peppers (diced)
	¼ cp. Onion (diced)
	1 cp. Beef Bouillon
	¼ cp. Plum Tomatoes (canned)
	2 ea. Garlic Cloves
	2 tbs. Fresh Basil

30% Fat:	2 tsp. Olive Oil

Method:
1) Prepare the polenta by following directions on box.
2) Sauté the minced onion and pepper in 1 tsp. olive oil and combine with the cooking polenta add the parmesan, pour on a plate, and let cool.
3) Sauté the veal scaloppini in remaining olive oil, adding the garlic, onions, peppers, basil, mushrooms, and tomatoes in that order. Braise for twenty minutes in the bouillon or until veal is fork tender.

Serving: Place the veal stew (cacciatore) over the polenta, serve heated.

Dinner Alternate: Chicken Cacciatore with Red Pepper Polenta
1) Omit veal and replace with boneless/skinless chicken thigh.

Nutrition Facts

1 Serving
Amount Per Serving

Calories	355.4
Total Fat	13.8 g
Saturated Fat	3.1 g
Polyunsaturated Fat	1.3 g
Monounsaturated Fat	8.0 g
Cholesterol	99.2 mg
Sodium	490.5 mg
Potassium	722.7 mg
Total Carbohydrate	28.2 g
Dietary Fiber	4.7 g
Sugars	1.5 g
Protein	29.6 g
Vitamin A	33.6 %
Vitamin B-12	29.4 %
Vitamin B-6	38.7 %
Vitamin C	105.2 %
Vitamin D	3.3 %
Vitamin E	10.1 %
Calcium	11.8 %
Copper	15.3 %
Folate	11.3 %
Iron	17.4 %
Magnesium	12.9 %
Manganese	16.6 %
Niacin	48.6 %
Pantothenic Acid	19.4 %
Phosphorus	34.0 %
Riboflavin	27.8 %
Selenium	19.8 %
Thiamin	13.4 %
Zinc	29.8 %

Day 2

Snack (Dessert)

Ginger Carrot Cake

Yield: 1 Serving

30% Protein:	1 tsp. Soy Protein Powder
	1 tb. Egg Substitute or Liquid Egg Whites
	2 tb. Buttermilk
	1 tb. Skim Milk
40% Carbohydrate:	6 tb. Whole Grain Flour
	1 tb. Soy Flour
	¼ tsp. Ground Ginger
	¼ tsp. Cinnamon Powder
	Pinch Baking Powder
	¼ tsp. Vanilla Extract
	1 tb. Brown Sugar
	¼ cp. Fresh Peeled Carrots (Shredded)
30% Fat:	2 tsp. Canola Oil

Suggestion: Prepare in advance, cool, and serve.

Method:
1) Combine all dry ingredients.
2) In a bowl whisk together until foamy the oil, egg substitute or egg whites.
3) Add the vanilla, brown sugar, and whisk until smooth.
4) Add the dairy ingredients, then all of the dry plus carrots.
5) Pour into an oiled 3" round tin or ceramic ramekin.
6) Bake in a 300 degree oven for twenty-five minutes or until top springs back when touched in middle.

Snack Alternate: Ginger Spice Cake
1) Omit carrots.

Nutrition Facts	
1 Serving	
Amount Per Serving	
Calories	91.9
Total Fat	4.8 g
Saturated Fat	0.5 g
Polyunsaturated Fat	1.4 g
Monounsaturated Fat	2.7 g
Cholesterol	0.8 mg
Sodium	195.4 mg
Potassium	105.8 mg
Total Carbohydrate	10.7 g
Dietary Fiber	0.9 g
Sugars	6.8 g
Protein	4.1 g
Vitamin A	11.3 %
Vitamin B-12	1.3 %
Vitamin B-6	1.7 %
Vitamin C	0.9 %
Vitamin D	0.6 %
Vitamin E	5.0 %
Calcium	6.8 %
Copper	4.0 %
Folate	4.9 %
Iron	4.5 %
Magnesium	4.0 %
Manganese	18.9 %
Niacin	1.5 %
Pantothenic Acid	1.3 %
Phosphorus	7.4 %
Riboflavin	4.4 %
Selenium	4.6 %
Thiamin	2.8 %
Zinc	2.6 %

Day 2

Mexican Egg Muffin with "Festive" Salsa Fresco

English muffin is a thin, round bread made with yeast dough and baked on a griddle. *Jack cheese* is a cooked and pressed cheese traditionally made in Monterey, California, from whole, skimmed or partly skimmed cow's milk. It has an ivory color, a semi-soft texture and varieties flavored with peppercorns, spices, herbs, or jalapenos.

Carb: English muffin, Scallions, Tomatoes, Onions, Cilantro, Peppers.
Protein: Egg Substitute, Pepper Jack Cheese.
Fat: Olive Oil

Turkey Salad Platter with Seedless Grapes and Yogurt-Dill Dressing

Dill is a member of the parsley family. It has tiny, aromatic, yellow flowers and feathery, delicate blue-green leaves. The leaves taste like parsley, but sharper, with a touch of anise. Both the seeds and leaves are used in cooking, commonly among Scandinavian and central European cuisines, particularly with fish and potatoes.

Carb: Grapes, Cucumber, Peppers, Onions, Celery, Mixed Greens
Protein: Turkey, Yogurt
Fat: Lite Mayonnaise

Brushetta with Roasted Garlic Puree and Melted Mozzarella

Brushetta is an Italian appetizer of toasted bread slices rubbed with garlic and drizzled with olive oil and sometimes topped with tomatoes and basil. In the United States, there is a variety in which it can be topped with olives, tomatoes, cheese, or other ingredients.

Carb: Bread, Garlic
Protein: Skim Mozzarella
Fat: Olive Oil

Veal Cacciatore with Red Pepper Polenta

Cacciatore is an Italian preparation method for meats stewed with tomatoes, onions, mushrooms, and various herbs and spices and sometimes wine. *Polenta* is an Italian dish comprised of cornmeal with a liquid, until it forms a soft mass. It is eaten hot or cooled, cut into squares, and grilled or fried.

Carb: Polenta, Peppers, Onion, Mushrooms, Tomatoes
Protein: Veal, Parmesan Cheese
Fat: Olive Oil

Day 2
Ingredient List

Dairy/Eggs:
4 oz. Egg Substitute
1 oz. Pepper jack Cheese
1 oz. Grated Parmesan
1 oz. Plain Yogurt
2 oz. Skim Mozzarella
1 oz. Buttermilk
1 oz. Skim Milk

Dry Goods:
1 ea. Whole Wheat English muffin
1 oz. Olive Oil
2 oz. Canned Plum Tomatoes
2 oz. Dry Polenta Mix
1 oz. Lite Mayonnaise
3 oz. Whole Grain Flour
1 oz. Soy Flour
1 oz. Powdered Ginger, Cinnamon
1 oz. Baking Powder
1 oz. Vanilla Extract
1 oz. Brown Sugar
1 oz. Canola Oil
1 oz. Soy Protein Powder
1 ea. Whole Grain French Roll
1 cn. Beef Bouillon

Meats:
3 oz. Deli Turkey
4 oz. Veal Cubes or Cutlet

Produce:
1 ea. Carrot
1 ea. Sm. Garlic Blub
1 ea. Celery Stalk
1 ea. Dill, Cilantro, Basil Sprig
4 cp. Mixed Salad Greens
4 oz. Grape Tomatoes
1 ea. Sm. Seedless Cucumber
1 ea. Stalk Scallion
1 ea. Red Onion, Sp. Onion
1 ea. Tomatillo (Green Tomato)
2 oz. Button Mushrooms
1 ea. Red, Green Pepper

Day 3

Breakfast

<u>Sweet Potato Pancakes with Scrambled Egg, Canadian Bacon Raspberry Maple Syrup</u>

Yield: 1 Serving

30% Protein:	2 oz. Egg Substitute or Liquid Egg Whites	
	2 oz. Slice Canadian Bacon	
	½ oz. Ricotta Cheese	

40% Carbohydrates:	¼ cp. Buttermilk Pancake Dry Mix
	1 oz. Raspberries
	1 tsp. Orange Rind (Optional)
	1 oz. Diet Maple Syrup
	2 Tb. Pulp of Baked Sweet Potato

30% Fat: 2 tsp. Canola oil

Method:
1) For pancakes: Combine pancake mix with ricotta, sweet potato pulp, and half the oil to make batter. In a non-stick skillet spoon 1 oz. ladles of batter and cook on both sides.
2) For syrup: In a food processor combine maple syrup, raspberries, and orange rind, puree.
3) For protein: Scramble 3 oz. egg substitute in remaining oil and grill the Canadian bacon.

Serving:
1) On a plate place pancakes, eggs, and turkey bacon.
2) Place the syrup in a 2 oz. soufflé container on the side.

Breakfast Alternate: Scrambled Egg Whites with Turkey Bacon and Country Potatoes

Yield: 1 Serving

30% Protein:	2 oz. Egg whites
	2 ea. Strips turkey bacon

40% Carbohydrate: 1 cp. Boiled potatoes

Nutrition Facts	
1 Serving	
Amount Per Serving	
Calories	406.4
Total Fat	18.2 g
Saturated Fat	3.2 g
Polyunsaturated Fat	6.0 g
Monounsaturated Fat	8.1 g
Cholesterol	78.8 mg
Sodium	1,118.4 mg
Potassium	501.7 mg
Total Carbohydrate	39.4 g
Dietary Fiber	0.7 g
Sugars	18.2 g
Protein	21.6 g
Vitamin A	17.7 %
Vitamin B-12	24.5 %
Vitamin B-6	11.8 %
Vitamin C	22.4 %
Vitamin D	10.0 %
Vitamin E	15.6 %
Calcium	15.6 %
Copper	9.9 %
Folate	23.0 %
Iron	20.1 %
Magnesium	7.7 %
Manganese	11.8 %
Niacin	11.6 %
Pantothenic Acid	17.4 %
Phosphorus	36.4 %
Riboflavin	67.3 %
Selenium	64.5 %
Thiamin	19.6 %
Zinc	17.6 %

　　　　　　　　1 sm. Chopped onion
　　　　　　　　¼ cp. Chopped green pepper

30% Fat:　　　　　　2 tsp. Olive oil

Method:
1) Scramble the eggs in half the oil.
2) Sauté the bacon, remove and reserve.
3) In the same pan with the bacon fat add the remaining oil and sauté the onion, peppers, and potatoes.

Serving: Place the eggs and bacon with the potatoes in microwaveable container accommodating

Day 3

Lunch

Grilled Portobello Napoleon

Yield: 1 Serving

30% Protein:	4 oz. or ½ cp. Shredded Skim Mozzarella Cheese

40% Carbohydrate:	2 ea. Medium Portobello Mushroom Caps
	2 ea. ½" thick slice of Japanese Eggplant
	2 ea. of ½" thick slice of Red, Yellow and Green Pepper
	2 ea. ½" thick slice of Red Onion
	2 ea. ½" thick slice of Beefsteak Tomato
	2 oz. or ¼ cp. Balsamic Vinegar
	2 tb. Fresh Basil (Chopped)

30% Fat:	2 tsp. Olive Oil

Method:
1) Rub vegetables in half the oil and grill or roast in a 350 degree oven until golden and tender, cool, and reserve.
2) Make dressing by combining remaining oil and vinegar.

Serving: Place on a plate the vegetables intermittently with mozzarella on top along with dressing, garnish with basil.

Lunch Alternate: Replace mozzarella with 3 ea./1 oz. slices of grilled chicken

Nutrition Facts	
1 Serving	
Amount Per Serving	
Calories	339.5
Total Fat	19.5 g
Saturated Fat	8.3 g
Polyunsaturated Fat	1.0 g
Monounsaturated Fat	6.7 g
Cholesterol	30.0 mg
Sodium	430.8 mg
Potassium	620.5 mg
Total Carbohydrate	25.1 g
Dietary Fiber	4.3 g
Sugars	1.0 g
Protein	17.2 g
Vitamin A	66.1 %
Vitamin B-12	0.5 %
Vitamin B-6	15.2 %
Vitamin C	159.6 %
Vitamin D	0.0 %
Vitamin E	8.7 %
Calcium	42.5 %
Copper	17.0 %
Folate	11.8 %
Iron	5.6 %
Magnesium	6.7 %
Manganese	15.3 %
Niacin	16.7 %
Pantothenic Acid	11.4 %
Phosphorus	11.9 %
Riboflavin	19.2 %
Selenium	9.9 %
Thiamin	9.5 %
Zinc	4.0 %

Day 3

Snack

Fresh Ahi Tuna and Garlic Aioli on Tortilla Chips

Yield: 1 Serving

		Nutrition Facts	

30% Protein: 2 ea. 1 oz. Medallions of Fresh Tuna

40% Carbohydrate: ½ pc. "Low Carb" Tortilla Wedges
(Toasted)
½ tsp. Garlic Cloves
½ tsp. Fresh Parsley (Minced)
2 tb. Roma Tomatoes (minced)
1 tb. Red Onion (Minced)

30% Fat: 1 tsp. Olive Oil

Method:
1) Grill the tuna medallions, reserve.
2) Toast the tortilla wedges.
3) In a processor, combine the garlic and parsley with the oil.

Serving:
1) Place the tuna on tortilla chips, spoon on aioli, and garnish
with the tomato and onion. Serve cold.

Snack Alternate: Grilled Chicken and Garlic Aioli on Tortilla
Chips
1) Omit the tuna and replace with 2 oz. grilled chicken.

Nutrition Facts

1 Serving
Amount Per Serving

Calories	173.9
Total Fat	6.7 g
Saturated Fat	1.1 g
Polyunsaturated Fat	0.6 g
Monounsaturated Fat	3.4 g
Cholesterol	32.9 mg
Sodium	182.7 mg
Potassium	407.0 mg
Total Carbohydrate	9.3 g
Dietary Fiber	4.7 g
Sugars	0.3 g
Protein	21.0 g
Vitamin A	4.6 %
Vitamin B-12	5.7 %
Vitamin B-6	31.2 %
Vitamin C	7.2 %
Vitamin D	0.0 %
Vitamin E	3.4 %
Calcium	9.0 %
Copper	3.8 %
Fol ate	1.9 %
Iron	5.8 %
Magnesium	10.2 %
Manganese	2.9 %
Niacin	34.9 %
Pantothenic Acid	5.8 %
Phosphorus	15.0 %
Riboflavin	2.9 %
Selenium	38.1 %
Thiamin	20.4 %
Zinc	2.9 %

Day 3

Dinner

Beef Bracciola with Roasted Tomato Sauce and Whole Grain Linguini

Yield: 1 Serving

30% Protein:	3 oz. Beef Top Round Steak (Sliced Thinly)
	½ tb. Parmesan Cheese (Grated)
40% Carbohydrate:	½ cp. Dry Whole Wheat Pasta (Linguini)
	3 ea. Plum Tomatoes
	3 ea. Garlic Cloves
	½ cp. Beef Broth
	1 tsp. Fresh Basil (Minced)
	¼ cp. Onion (Diced)
30% Fat:	2 tsp. Olive Oil

Method:

Suggestion: Steps 1-2 can be done in advance and reserved in the refrigerator.

1) Roll the parmesan in the beef and tie with string to close.
2) In a sauté pan with 1 tsp. oil sear the beef roll with the onions and reserve when brown on all sides.
3) Cut the tomatoes in half and place on a sheet pan with the garlic cloves. Roast in a 350 degree oven until all is tender and caramelized.
4) When tomatoes are finished place in a bake-able dish, add the beef broth and the beef roll, surround with onions and basil.
5) Braise all in the tomato sauce at 350 degrees for ½ hour or until the beef roll is tender.
6) In a pot of salted boiling water place the pasta and cook al dente to the touch.

Serving:
1) Place the pasta, sauce, and Bracciola on a plate and serve heated.

Dinner Alternate: Turkey Bracciola with Roasted Tomato Sauce
1) Omit the beef and replace with fresh turkey cutlet.

Nutrition Facts	
1 Serving	
Amount Per Serving	
Calories	425.5
Total Fat	17.9 g
Saturated Fat	4.6 g
Polyunsaturated Fat	1.5 g
Monounsaturated Fat	10.0 g
Cholesterol	77.6 mg
Sodium	515.4 mg
Potassium	952.6 mg
Total Carbohydrate	33.8 g
Dietary Fiber	6.1 g
Sugars	0.1 g
Protein	34.6 g
Vitamin A	23.5 %
Vitamin B-12	42.4 %
Vitamin B-6	37.9 %
Vitamin C	39.9 %
Vitamin D	0.0 %
Vitamin E	10.2 %
Calcium	9.5 %
Copper	21.5 %
Folate	12.6 %
Iron	27.4 %
Magnesium	19.6 %
Manganese	69.6 %
Niacin	31.8 %
Pantothenic Acid	12.2 %
Phosphorus	37.7 %
Riboflavin	24.7 %
Selenium	71.2 %
Thiamin	22.3 %
Zinc	43.6 %

Day 3

Snack (Dessert)

White and Dark Chocolate Chip Cookies

Yield: 1 Serving

30% Protein:	2 tb. Liquid Egg Whites
	1 tb. Soy Protein Powder

40% Carbohydrate:	¼ cp. AP Whole Grain Flour
	1 tb. Soy Flour
	¼ cp. Brown Sugar
	¼ tsp. Vanilla Extract
	Pinch Baking Soda
	1 tsp. Dark Chocolate Chips
	1 tsp. White Chocolate Chips

30% Fat:	2 tb. Soy Butter or Unsalted/Sweet Butter

Suggestion: Prepare in advance, cool, and serve.

Method:
1) In a mixer or bowl, cream the butter with the sugar.
2) Beat in the eggs and vanilla.
3) Add all dry ingredients including the chocolate and fold together forming dough.
4) Scoop out for 2 ea. cookie dough and flatten.
5) Bake at 300 degrees for twenty minutes or until golden and done.

Serving:
1) Place two cookies on a paper doily and serve cooled or hot.

Snack Alternate: White and Dark Raisin Cookies
1) Omit the chocolate and replace with raisins.

Nutrition Facts	
2 Servings	
Amount Per Serving	
Calories	101.7
Total Fat	4.6 g
Saturated Fat	2.2 g
Polyunsaturated Fat	0.8 g
Monounsaturated Fat	1.5 g
Cholesterol	0.0 mg
Sodium	172.5 mg
Potassium	109.2 mg
Total Carbohydrate	14.4 g
Dietary Fiber	1.3 g
Sugars	9.8 g
Protein	3.9 g
Vitamin A	1.1 %
Vitamin B-12	1.5 %
Vitamin B-6	1.5 %
Vitamin C	0.0 %
Vitamin D	0.7 %
Vitamin E	1.1 %
Calcium	2.4 %
Copper	7.1 %
Folate	5.2 %
Iron	5.6 %
Magnesium	6.3 %
Manganese	19.5 %
Niacin	1.6 %
Pantothenic Acid	1.3 %
Phosphorus	6.6 %
Riboflavin	5.5 %
Selenium	6.0 %
Thiamin	3.1 %
Zinc	3.3 %

Day 3

Sweet Potato Pancakes with Scrambled Eggs and Raspberry Maple Syrup

Ricotta is a cheese made from the whey remaining after other cow's milk cheeses have been made. It has a somewhat grainy texture and a slightly sweet flavor. It is a good source of protein, calcium, and selenium.

Carb: Yam, Pancake Mix, Raspberries, Maple Syrup
Protein: Egg Whites, Turkey Bacon, and Ricotta Cheese
Fat: Olive Oil

Grilled Portobello Napoleon with Buffalo Mozzarella

Buffalo Mozzarella is a cheese made from water buffalo's milk that has a white color and a mild, delicate flavor used mostly for cooking.

Carb: Mushroom, Eggplant, Peppers, Onion, Tomato
Protein: Skim Mozzarella
Fat: Olive Oil

Fresh Ahi Tuna with Garlic Aioli and Tortilla Chips

Aioli is a garlic mayonnaise made in France's provinces region. It is used as a condiment or sauce.

Carb: Corn chips, Tomatoes, Garlic
Protein: Tuna
Fat: Olive Oil

Beef Bracciola with Roasted Tomato Sauce and Whole Wheat Linguini

Tomatoes, although technically a fruit, are usually prepared as vegetables. They are high in vitamin C and beta carotene. *Bracciola* is Italian for a slice or chop of meat, often stuffed.

Carb: Pasta, Tomatoes, Onions
Protein: Beef
Fat: Olive Oil

Day 3
Ingredient List

Dairy/Eggs:
2 oz. Egg Substitute
1 oz. Skim Ricotta Cheese
1 oz. Grated Parmesan Cheese
4 oz. Skim Mozzarella Cheese
1 oz. Liquid Egg Whites
1 oz. Soy Butter or Unsalted/Sweet Butter

Dry Goods:
2 oz. Dry Buttermilk Pancake Mix
1 oz. Diet Maple Syrup
1 oz. Canola Oil
2 oz. Olive Oil
2 oz. Dry Whole Wheat Linguini
2 oz. Beef Broth
2 oz. Balsamic Vinegar
1 ea. 6" Low Carb Tortilla
2 oz. Whole Grain Flour
1 oz. Soy Flour
2 oz. Brown Sugar
½ oz. Vanilla Extract
½ oz. Baking Soda
½ oz. ea. White, Dark Chocolate Chips

Meats/Seafood:
2 oz. Pork Canadian Bacon
4 oz. Beef Top Round Cutlet
2 oz. Ahi Tuna

Produce:
1 oz. Fresh Raspberries
1 ea. Sm. Orange
1 ea. Sm. Yam
4 ea. Plum Tomatoes
3 ea. Garlic Cloves
1 ea. Basil, Parsley Sprig
1 ea. Sm. Sp. Onion
1 ea. Japanese Eggplant
1 ea. Red, Green, Yellow Peppers
1 ea. Red Onion

Day 4

Breakfast

Hawaii Breakfast Cereal with Sugar Banana

Yield: 1 Serving

30% Protein:	1 cp. Skim Milk
	2 tb. Vanilla Whey Protein Powder
	(Muscle Milk Brand Preferred)

40% Carbohydrate:	¾ cp. Cooked Brown Rice
	1 tb. Raisins (Dark)
	¼ tsp. Ground Cinnamon
	1 tb. Honey
	½ tsp. Banana or Vanilla Extract
	1 ea. Sm. Sugar Banana (Sliced)

30% Fat:	2 tsp. Chopped Macadamia Nuts (Toasted)

Method:
1) In a sauce pot, combine the cooked rice with the milk, raisins, and cinnamon and simmer until heated.
2) Remove from heat and stir in the protein powder.
3) Place the sliced banana in honey.

Serving:
1) Place cooked cereal in a bowl and top with the banana and honey. Garnish with the nuts.

Breakfast Alternate: Country Breakfast Cereal with Strawberries
1) Omit the rice and replace with toasted barley.
2) Omit the banana and replace with ¼ cp. strawberries.
3) Omit the nuts and replace with 2 tsp. soy butter.

Nutrition Facts	
1 Serving	
Amount Per Serving	
Calories	400.6
Total Fat	11.2 g
Saturated Fat	4.2 g
Polyunsaturated Fat	0.5 g
Monounsaturated Fat	5.3 g
Cholesterol	5.0 mg
Sodium	142.1 mg
Potassium	299.9 mg
Total Carbohydrate	65.3 g
Dietary Fiber	3.4 g
Sugars	32.0 g
Protein	12.6 g
Vitamin A	12.8 %
Vitamin B-12	2.2 %
Vitamin B-6	5.5 %
Vitamin C	9.8 %
Vitamin D	25.0 %
Vitamin E	5.7 %
Calcium	35.3 %
Copper	6.7 %
Folate	1.4 %
Iron	8.8 %
Magnesium	5.8 %
Manganese	19.0 %
Niacin	3.4 %
Pantothenic Acid	1.0 %
Phosphorus	6.0 %
Riboflavin	5.4 %
Selenium	2.6 %
Thiamin	8.1 %
Zinc	3.6 %

Day 4

Lunch

Grilled Veggie Quesadilla

Yield: 1 Serving

30% Protein:	4 oz. or ½ cp. Colby Cheese (Shredded)
40% Carbohydrate:	¼ cp. Red Bell Pepper (Sliced)
	¼ cp. Red Onion (Sliced)
	¼ cp. Yellow Squash (Sliced)
	¼ cp. Zucchini (Sliced)
	1 ea. 6" Low-Carb Wrap
30% Fat:	2 tsp. Olive Oil

Method:
1) Toss all vegetables in oil and grill or roast in hot oven.
2) On half of the tortilla top with vegetables.
3) Cover with cheese and place other half of tortilla on top. Bake at 300 degree oven, until cheese melts.

Serving:
1) Cut quesadilla half into wedges and place on a plate.

Lunch Alternate: Grilled Veggie and Chicken Quesadilla
1) Omit the cheese and replace with 4 oz. grilled chicken.

Nutrition Facts	
1 Serving	
Amount Per Serving	
Calories	412.7
Total Fat	19.9 g
Saturated Fat	6.8 g
Polyunsaturated Fat	1.1 g
Monounsaturated Fat	9.0 g
Cholesterol	23.8 mg
Sodium	1,215.5 mg
Potassium	472.5 mg
Total Carbohydrate	27.1 g
Dietary Fiber	10.4 g
Sugars	2.7 g
Protein	36.5 g
Vitamin A	27.5 %
Vitamin B-12	9.3 %
Vitamin B-6	17.0 %
Vitamin C	81.4 %
Vitamin D	0.0 %
Vitamin E	9.8 %
Calcium	64.6 %
Copper	7.7 %
Folate	12.6 %
Iron	11.1 %
Magnesium	11.0 %
Manganese	15.7 %
Niacin	5.1 %
Pantothenic Acid	6.5 %
Phosphorus	61.0 %
Riboflavin	19.8 %
Selenium	24.3 %
Thiamin	6.3 %
Zinc	16.6 %

Day 4

Snack

Spaghetti Squash with Mozzarella, Tomatoes, and Basil Vinaigrette

Yield: 1 Serving

30% Protein:	2 oz. Bocconcini Mozzarella Balls or Slice
40% Carbohydrate:	½ cp. Cooked Spaghetti Squash (cook by boiling a half small squash in water until tender)
	¼ cp. Fresh Plum Tomatoes (Diced)
	1 tb. Balsamic Vinegar
	1 tsp. Fresh Basil (Chopped)
30% Fat:	½ tsp. Olive Oil

Method:
1) In a bowl combine the tomatoes with the vinegar and basil. Toss and reserve.
2) Cool and then shred the squash with a fork.

Serving:
1) Place the cooked shredded squash on a plate and top with the tomato mixture.
2) Top with the mozzarella balls or slice.
3) Serve chilled.

Snack Alternate: Zucchini Squash with Mozzarella, Tomatoes, and Basil Vinaigrette
1) Omit the spaghetti squash and replace with sliced roasted zucchini.

Nutrition Facts	
1 Serving	
Amount Per Serving	
Calories	192.8
Total Fat	11.5 g
Saturated Fat	6.1 g
Polyunsaturated Fat	0.6 g
Monounsaturated Fat	4.2 g
Cholesterol	32.9 mg
Sodium	283.2 mg
Potassium	138.3 mg
Total Carbohydrate	8.6 g
Dietary Fiber	1.1 g
Sugars	2.0 g
Protein	14.3 g
Vitamin A	8.3 %
Vitamin B-12	7.7 %
Vitamin B-6	5.8 %
Vitamin C	4.5 %
Vitamin D	0.0 %
Vitamin E	3.1 %
Calcium	38.3 %
Copper	2.1 %
Folate	2.8 %
Iron	2.2 %
Magnesium	5.4 %
Manganese	4.5 %
Niacin	3.4 %
Pantothenic Acid	3.2 %
Phosphorus	27.3 %
Riboflavin	11.1 %
Selenium	12.0 %
Thiamin	2.6 %
Zinc	11.5 %

Day 4

Dinner

Maple Marinated Grilled Pork Loin with Pecan Rice

Yield: 1 Serving

30% Protein:	4 ea. / 1 oz. Pork Loin Medallions

40% Carbohydrate:	1 tbsp. 'Diet' Maple Syrup
	¼ cp. Lg. Diced Fennel
	¼ cp. Lg. Diced Red Onion
	¼ cp. Lg. Diced Pineapple
	1 tbsp. Jerk Seasoning
	6 ea. Dried Bay Leaves
	½ cp. Cooked Brown Rice

30% Fat:	2 tsp. Olive Oil

Method:
1) Marinate the pork medallions in the combine oil, jerk seasoning, and syrup.
2) Make two skewers of each pork, fennel, vegetables, fruit, and bay leaves.
3) Grill until pork is well done and syrup is caramelized.

Serving:
1) Place the pecan rice on a plate and lay the skewers over.

Dinner Alternate: "Port Au Prince" Maple Marinated Chicken with Basmati Rice
1) Omit the pork and replace with 4 ea. 1 oz. chicken breast medallions.
2) Omit the pecan rice and replace with basmati rice.
3) Omit the walnut oil and replace with olive oil.

Nutrition Facts	
1 Serving	
Amount Per Serving	
Calories	472.8
Total Fat	17.5 g
Saturated Fat	3.6 g
Polyunsaturated Fat	6.4 g
Monounsaturated Fat	5.0 g
Cholesterol	106.5 mg
Sodium	128.9 mg
Potassium	875.3 mg
Total Carbohydrate	40.6 g
Dietary Fiber	4.3 g
Sugars	8.9 g
Protein	37.9 g
Vitamin A	1.5 %
Vitamin B-12	18.9 %
Vitamin B-6	34.9 %
Vitamin C	24.8 %
Vitamin D	0.0 %
Vitamin E	1.9 %
Calcium	3.8 %
Copper	8.6 %
Folate	7.6 %
Iron	13.1 %
Magnesium	14.4 %
Manganese	40.2 %
Niacin	31.6 %
Pantothenic Acid	12.5 %
Phosphorus	37.8 %
Riboflavin	28.0 %
Selenium	84.7 %
Thiamin	78.5 %
Zinc	23.6 %

Day 4

Snack (Dessert)

Almond Fruit Bars

Yield: 1 Serving

30% Protein:	2Tb. Soy Protein Powder
40% Carbohydrate:	¼ cp. Graham Cracker Crumbs
	1Tb. Soy Flour
	2Tb. Ground Rolled Oats
	1Tb. Brown Sugar
	¼ cp. Apricot Preserves
30% Fat:	2Tb. Soy Butter
	1Tb. Crushed Almonds

Suggestion: Prepare a day in advance, cool and reserve.

Method:
1) To make the crust put all ingredients (but the apricot preserves) in a bowl or mixer and paddle until combined.
2) Press into a greased 3" pastry tin or ceramic ramekin and bake at 275 degrees for 25 min. until golden brown, let cool.
3) Cover with the preserves and bake further at 275 degrees until preserves bubble, let cool and reserve.

Serve: 'As Is' in ramekin or tin

Snack Alternate: Apricot Fruit Bars
1) Omit the almonds.

Nutrition Facts	
1 Serving	
Amount Per Serving	
Calories	189.4
Total Fat	12.5 g
Saturated Fat	3.4 g
Polyunsaturated Fat	4.1 g
Monounsaturated Fat	4.5 g
Cholesterol	0.0 mg
Sodium	208.0 mg
Potassium	133.8 mg
Total Carbohydrate	18.3 g
Dietary Fiber	2.0 g
Sugars	5.8 g
Protein	5.8 g
Vitamin A	0.1 %
Vitamin B-12	0.0 %
Vitamin B-6	1.7 %
Vitamin C	0.0 %
Vitamin D	0.0 %
Vitamin E	4.7 %
Calcium	3.7 %
Copper	9.7 %
Folate	8.2 %
Iron	8.5 %
Magnesium	9.7 %
Manganese	38.8 %
Niacin	3.3 %
Pantothenic Acid	1.9 %
Phosphorus	11.7 %
Riboflavin	5.2 %
Selenium	1.9 %
Thiamin	7.3 %
Zinc	5.2 %

Day 4

Country Breakfast Cereal with Bananas and Honey
Carb: Brown Rice, Raisins, Honey, bananas, Oats
Protein: Skim Milk, Protein Powder
Fat: Almonds

Grilled Veggie and Monterey Jack Quesadilla
Quesadilla is a Mexican and American Southwestern dish of a flour tortilla filled with cheese and sometimes meat, chicken, refried beans, or the like, folded in half and grilled.
Carb: Peppers, Onions, Squash, Zucchini, Wrap
Protein: Jack Cheese
Fat: Olive Oil

Spaghetti Squash with Mozzarella, Tomatoes, and Basil Vinaigrette
Spaghetti squash is a large watermelon-shaped winter squash with a creamy yellow shell. It has a slightly nutty-flavored flesh that separates into yellow-gold spaghetti-like strands when cooked. *Bocconcini* is fresh mozzarella cheese shaped into small balls about one inch in diameter.
Carb: Spaghetti Squash, Plum Tomatoes
Protein: Bocconcini Mozzarella
Fat: Olive Oil

"Port Au Prince" Maple Marinated Pork Loin with Pecan Rice
Carb: Diet Maple Syrup, Fennel, Onion, Pineapple, Pecan Rice
Protein: Pork
Fat: Walnut Oil

Day 4

Ingredient List

<u>Dairy/Eggs:</u>
8 oz. Skim Milk
4 oz. Colby Cheese or Monterey Jack
2 oz. Fresh Mozzarella Bocconcini Balls or Slices
1 oz. Soy Butter or Unsalted/Sweet Butter

<u>Dry Goods:</u>
1 oz. Vanilla Whey Protein Powder
½ oz. Dark Raisins
½ oz. Powdered Cinnamon
½ oz. Honey
½ oz. Vanilla or Banana Extract
½ oz. Macadamia Nuts, Almonds
4 oz. Dry Brown Rice
½ oz. Diet Maple Syrup
½ oz. Dry Jerk Seasoning
1 oz. Olive Oil
1 ea. 6" Low Carb Wheat Tortilla
1 oz. Balsamic Vinegar
2 oz. Graham Cracker Crumbs
1 oz. Rolled or Ground Oats
1 oz. Brown Sugar
2 oz. Apricot Preserves

<u>Meats:</u>
4 oz. Pork Loin (Boneless)

<u>Produce:</u>
1 ea. Sm. Sugar Banana
2 ea. Bulbs Fennel
1 ea. Red Onion
½ ea. Pineapple
1 ea. Red Pepper
1 ea. Sm. Zucchini, Yellow Squash
1 ea. Spaghetti Squash
2 ea. Plum Tomatoes
1 ea. Sprig Basil

Day 5

Breakfast

Pumpernickel "Mini" Bagel with Smoked Nova Salmon, Red Onion, and Capers

Yield: 1 Serving

30% Protein:	2 oz. Smoked Nova Salmon Lox
	1 ea. Hard-Boiled Egg
40% Carbohydrate:	1 ea. Mini Bagel or Half of Whole
	1 tb. Red Onion (Minced)
	1 tsp. Capers
30% Fat:	1 tb. Plain "Lite" Cream Cheese

Method:
1) Slice bagel and toast.
2) Slice hard-boiled egg.

Serving:
1) Place salmon on a plate and garnish with egg, capers, and onion.
2) Spread cream cheese on the bagel

Breakfast Alternate: Pumpernickel "Mini" Bagel with Hard-Boiled Egg
1) Omit salmon and replace with 2 ea. hard-boiled eggs sliced in half while retaining the yolks.

Nutrition Facts	
1 Serving	
Amount Per Serving	
Calories	366.1
Total Fat	10.7 g
Saturated Fat	2.9 g
Polyunsaturated Fat	1.6 g
Monounsaturated Fat	3.9 g
Cholesterol	233.8 mg
Sodium	2,339.8 mg
Potassium	609.6 mg
Total Carbohydrate	36.6 g
Dietary Fiber	7.4 g
Sugars	17.5 g
Protein	33.4 g
Vitamin A	20.1 %
Vitamin B-12	58.0 %
Vitamin B-6	21.7 %
Vitamin C	164.8 %
Vitamin D	0.0 %
Vitamin E	5.2 %
Calcium	19.5 %
Copper	16.9 %
Folate	23.3 %
Iron	14.5 %
Magnesium	11.6 %
Manganese	5.5 %
Niacin	23.4 %
Pantothenic Acid	19.7 %
Phosphorus	37.7 %
Riboflavin	28.1 %
Selenium	71.8 %
Thiamin	15.5 %
Zinc	8.0 %

Day 5

Lunch

Catalina Chicken Salad with Mango and Cranraisins

Yield: 1 Serving

30% Protein:	4 oz. Boneless Chicken Thigh
40% Carbohydrate:	4 cps. Mesclun Salad Greens
	1 tb. Cranraisins
	¼ cp. Fresh Mango (Diced)
	1 tb. Celery (Diced)
	2 tb. Catalina Dressing (Kraft Brand)
	1 tb. Red Onion (Diced)
	¼ cp. Grape Tomatoes
	¼ cp. Cucumber (Coin Cut)
30% Fat:	1 tb. Diet Mayonnaise

Method:
1) Marinate the chicken thigh in half the Catalina dressing and then grill.
2) Dice the chicken and combine the mayonnaise with the mango, onions, celery, and the remaining dressing.

Serving:
1) Place the greens in a bowl and top with the grilled Catalina chicken salad.
2) Surround with tomatoes and cucumbers.
3) Garnish with the Cranraisins.

Lunch Alternate: Grilled Chicken Salad with Raspberry Vinaigrette
1) Omit the Catalina dressing.
2) Omit the mango and Cranraisins. Replace with diced carrots.

Nutrition Facts	
1 Serving	
Amount Per Serving	
Calories	400.8
Total Fat	19.9 g
Saturated Fat	3.0 g
Polyunsaturated Fat	0.8 g
Monounsaturated Fat	0.9 g
Cholesterol	62.5 mg
Sodium	370.6 mg
Potassium	396.7 mg
Total Carbohydrate	23.9 g
Dietary Fiber	3.7 g
Sugars	16.2 g
Protein	16.5 g
Vitamin A	133.1 %
Vitamin B-12	4.0 %
Vitamin B-6	17.4 %
Vitamin C	69.0 %
Vitamin D	0.0 %
Vitamin E	7.3 %
Calcium	6.3 %
Copper	7.6 %
Folate	6.7 %
Iron	14.1 %
Magnesium	7.5 %
Manganese	5.5 %
Niacin	24.5 %
Pantothenic Acid	11.1 %
Phosphorus	15.0 %
Riboflavin	10.9 %
Selenium	14.1 %
Thiamin	7.8 %
Zinc	9.7 %

Day 5

Snack

Wilted Spinach and "Hearty" Cheese Dip

Yield: 1 Serving

30% Protein:	1 oz. Feta Cheese
	1 tb. Grated Parmesan
	¼ cp. Skim Milk
40% Carbohydrate:	2 cp. Spinach Leaves
	½ cp. or 2 ea. Artichoke Hearts (Canned)
30% Fat:	1½ tsp. Bleu Cheese (Crumbled)

Method:
1) Steam spinach until just tender. Cool and reserve.
2) In a separate sauce pot combine cheeses with skim milk and melt over low heat, stirring so as not to scorch bottom until a thickened sauce is formed.

Serving:
1) Place artichoke hearts over spinach on a plate and top with cheese mixture.

Snack Alternate: Wilted Spinach with Kasha and Feta Cheese
1) Replace all other cheese with 2 oz. feta.
2) Replace artichoke hearts with ½ cp. kasha (Buck wheat groats).

Nutrition Fact	
1 Serving	
Amount Per Serving	
Calories	178.0
Total Fat	9.5 g
Saturated Fat	6.1 g
Polyunsaturated Fat	0.5 g
Monounsaturated Fat	2.2 g
Cholesterol	20.3 mg
Sodium	405.7 mg
Potassium	1,025.1 mg
Total Carbohydrate	12.2 g
Dietary Fiber	6.8 g
Sugars	1.1 g
Protein	14.8 g
Vitamin A	386.6 %
Vitamin B-12	2.9 %
Vitamin B-6	28.7 %
Vitamin C	35.0 %
Vitamin D	0.0 %
Vitamin E	9.5 %
Calcium	36.8 %
Copper	27.9 %
Folate	87.3 %
Iron	40.7 %
Magnesium	45.3 %
Manganese	93.4 %
Niacin	8.2 %
Pantothenic Acid	7.1 %
Phosphorus	25.8 %
Riboflavin	38.7 %
Selenium	7.6 %
Thiamin	15.4 %
Zinc	14.0 %

Day 5

Dinner

Roasted Lamb Top Round with Garlicky Potatoes and Broccoli Rape

Yield: 1 Serving

30% Protein: 4 oz. Lamb Top Round Stew or Roast
1 tb. Parmesan Cheese (Grated)

40% Carbohydrate: ½ cp. Red Bliss Potato (Thinly sliced)
2 cp. Broccoli Rape or Broccoli
¼ tsp. Nutmeg (Grated)
¼ tsp. Garlic Powder

30% Fat: ½ cp. Half and Half
1 tsp. Olive Oil

Method:
1) Combine potato, nutmeg, garlic, parmesan, and half and half.
2) In a covered roasting tin or ceramic ramekin bake at 350 degrees until potatoes are tender.
3) Rub and season the lamb with the olive and a pinch of garlic powder, salt, and pepper. Roast in the oven in a separate pan, until at least medium rare.
4) In a sauce pot of simmering salted water cook the vegetable until tender.

Serving:
1) Place the potatoes and broccoli rape on a plate with the lamb.

Dinner Alternate: Baked Salmon with Garlicky Potatoes and Baby Spinach
1) Omit the lamb and replace with 6 oz. salmon fillet.
2) Replace the broccoli rape with fresh spinach.

Nutrition Facts	
1 Serving	
Amount Per Serving	
Calories	381.6
Total Fat	9.1 g
Saturated Fat	4.0 g
Polyunsaturated Fat	0.7 g
Monounsaturated Fat	3.2 g
Cholesterol	79.5 mg
Sodium	344.9 mg
Potassium	1,591.4 mg
Total Carbohydrate	43.0 g
Dietary Fiber	8.4 g
Sugars	6.4 g
Protein	33.6 g
Vitamin A	62.7 %
Vitamin B-12	63.3 %
Vitamin B-6	62.9 %
Vitamin C	218.7 %
Vitamin D	0.0 %
Vitamin E	13.5 %
Calcium	21.6 %
Copper	24.5 %
Folate	48.8 %
Iron	22.9 %
Magnesium	26.4 %
Manganese	27.5 %
Niacin	44.2 %
Pantothenic Acid	23.1 %
Phosphorus	53.9 %
Riboflavin	45.0 %
Selenium	16.0 %
Thiamin	28.7 %
Zinc	44.0 %

Day 5

Snack (Dessert)

Pumpkin Cheese Cake Soufflé

Yield: 1 Serving

Suggestion: Prepare a day in advance, refrigerate, and reserve.

Crust:

30% Protein:	1 tb. Soy Protein Powder
40% Carbohydrate:	1 tb. Brown Sugar
	1 tsp. Soy Flour
	2 tb. Ground Oats
	1 tb. Whole Grain Flour
30% Fat:	1 tb. Soy Butter

Method:
1) In a mixer or bowl combine all crust ingredients on low speed until incorporated. Place into the bottom of a cupcake liner that has been inserted into a muffin tin.

Filling:

30% Protein:	4 tb. Cottage Cheese
	2 tsp. Egg Substitute or Liquid Egg Whites
	1 tb. Half & Half
40% Carbohydrate:	2 tb. Pumpkin Puree
	1 tsp. Granulated Sugar (Preferably Fructose)
	¼ tsp. Cinnamon
	¼ tsp. Nutmeg
	Pinch Baking Powder
30% Fat:	1 tb. Low Fat Cream Cheese

Method:
1) Puree the cottage cheese with the half & half in a blender add the remaining ingredients.
2) Pour over the crust and bake at 300 degrees until set, chill in refrigerator.

Serving:
1) "As is" placed on a plate.

Snack Alternate: Sweet Potato Cheesecake Bars
1) Omit pumpkin and replace with canned yams.

Nutrition Facts	
1 Serving	
Amount Per Serving	
Calories	102.1
Total Fat	3.5 g
Saturated Fat	1.2 g
Polyunsaturated Fat	1.1 g
Monounsaturated Fat	1.1 g
Cholesterol	6.4 mg
Sodium	299.0 mg
Potassium	74.3 mg
Total Carbohydrate	9.1 g
Dietary Fiber	0.5 g
Sugars	4.8 g
Protein	9.6 g
Vitamin A	5.5 %
Vitamin B-12	4.8 %
Vitamin B-6	2.0 %
Vitamin C	0.3 %
Vitamin D	0.4 %
Vitamin E	0.6 %
Calcium	9.7 %
Copper	3.3 %
Folate	4.0 %
Iron	2.9 %
Magnesium	3.1 %
Manganese	11.9 %
Niacin	0.9 %
Pantothenic Acid	1.5 %
Phosphorus	6.8 %
Riboflavin	5.7 %
Selenium	6.5 %
Thiamin	3.0 %
Zinc	2.6 %

Day 5

Pumpernickel Mini Bagel with Smoked Salmon, Red Onion and Capers

Capers are the unopened flower buds of a shrub native to the Mediterranean region. After curing in salted white vinegar, the buds develop a sharp, salty-sour flavor and are used for flavoring and as a condiment.

Carb: Bagel, Pickled Cauliflower and Carrots, Red Onion, Capers
Protein: Salmon, Egg
Fat: Lite Cream Cheese

Catalina Chicken Salad with Mango and Cranraisins

Catalina is a tomato based dressing that has a sweet flavor. *Cranraisins* are dried cranberries that are sweetened to offset the natural sourness of the cranberry.

Carb: Cranraisins, Mango, Celery, Onions, Tomatoes, Cucumber
Protein: Chicken
Fat: Olive Oil

Wilted Spinach and Hearty Cheese Dip

Farmer cheese is an American cottage cheese-style cheese made from whole or partly skimmed cow's milk; generally eaten fresh, it has a soft texture (but is firm enough to slice or crumble), a milky white appearance, and a slightly tangy flavor. Also known as pressed cheese.

Carb: Spinach, Artichoke Hearts
Protein: Farmers Cheese, Parmesan Cheese
Fat: Blue Cheese

Baked Leg of Lamb with Garlicky Potatoes and Baby Spinach

Lamb is quite tender and can be prepared by almost any cooking method. It has a strong and distinctive flavor and goes well with boldly flavored sauces and accompaniments.

Carb: Red Bliss Potato, Baby Spinach, Garlic
Protein: Lamb, Parmesan Cheese
Fat: Half & Half

Day 5
Ingredient List

Dairy/Eggs:
1 ea. Whole Egg
1 oz. Low Fat Cream Cheese
1 oz. Feta Cheese
1 oz. Grated Parmesan
2 oz. Skim Milk
2 oz. Cottage Cheese
½ oz. Soy Butter or Unsalted/Sweet Butter
½ oz. Egg Substitute
2 oz. Non Fat Half & Half
½ oz. Crumbled Blue Cheese

Dry Goods:
1 ea. Mini Bagel or ½ of Whole
½ oz. Capers
½ oz. Cranraisins
1 oz. Kraft Catalina Dressing
1 oz. Lite Mayonnaise
1 ea. Sm. Can Artichoke Hearts
½ oz. Olive Oil
¼ oz. Ground Nutmeg, Cinnamon, Garlic Powder
½ oz. Soy Protein Powder
½ oz. Brown Sugar
½ oz. Soy Flour
1 oz. Rolled or Ground Oats
1 oz. Whole Grain Flour
1 oz. Canned Pumpkin Puree
½ oz. Granulated Sugar (Fructose Preferred)
¼ oz. Baking Powder

Seafood/Meats:
2 oz. Smoked Salmon (Lox)
4 oz. Boneless/Skinless Chicken Thigh
4 oz. Lamb Top Round Stew or Roast

Produce:
1 ea. Sm. Sugar Banana
2 ea. Bulbs Fennel
1 ea. Red Onion
½ ea. Pineapple
1 ea. Red Pepper
1 ea. Sm. Zucchini, Yellow Squash
1 ea. Spaghetti Squash
2 ea. Plum Tomatoes
1 ea. Sprig Basil

Day 6

Breakfast

Scrambled Eggs on English Muffin with Ham and Sautéed Spinach, Choron Sauce

Yield: 1 Serving

30% Protein:	3 oz. Egg Substitute or 2 ea. Whole Eggs (yolk has cholesterol) 1 oz./2 ea. Slice of Ham (Sautéed) ¼ cp. Non Fat Half & Half
40% Carbohydrate:	1 ea. Whole Wheat English Muffin (Toasted) 1 cp. Chopped Spinach ½ tsp. Tomato paste
30% Fat:	1 tsp. Canola Oil ¼ cp. Non Fat Half & Half

Method:
1) Scramble the egg substitute in ½ tsp. oil, reserve.
2) Sauté the spinach separately in ½ tsp. oil, reserve.
3) In a sauce pot simmer the half & half and tomato paste, reduce by half to make Choron sauce.

Serving:
1) Divide the ingredients between the muffins and place the eggs, ham, and spinach in that order.
2) Pour the sauce over.

Breakfast Alternate: Scrambled Eggs with Turkey Ham and Sautéed Spinach
1) Omit the pork ham and replace with turkey ham.

Nutrition Facts	
1 Serving	
Amount Per Serving	
Calories	346.9
Total Fat	11.1 g
Saturated Fat	2.9 g
Polyunsaturated Fat	2.2 g
Monounsaturated Fat	4.9 g
Cholesterol	35.1 mg
Sodium	1,754.0 mg
Potassium	1,852.3 mg
Total Carbohydrate	30.5 g
Dietary Fiber	7.2 g
Sugars	7.5 g
Protein	33.8 g
Vitamin A	420.4 %
Vitamin B-12	48.7 %
Vitamin B-6	50.9 %
Vitamin C	41.7 %
Vitamin D	23.1 %
Vitamin E	30.0 %
Calcium	40.5 %
Copper	28.0 %
Folate	102.5 %
Iron	60.7 %
Magnesium	50.7 %
Manganese	105.0 %
Niacin	28.7 %
Pantothenic Acid	28.1 %
Phosphorus	45.0 %
Riboflavin	141.6 %
Selenium	75.9 %
Thiamin	76.5 %
Zinc	28.4 %

Day 6

Lunch

Crab Salad with Melon and Herbed Mayonnaise

Yield: 1 Serving

30% Protein:	4 oz. Cooked Crabmeat (Canned Blue Claw)

40% Carbohydrate:	4 cps. Lettuce Greens
	½ tb. Chili Sauce
	¼ tsp. Dried Tarragon
	¼ tsp. Dried Basil
	¼ tsp. Garlic Powder
	½ cp. Red/Yellow Peppers (Diced)
	¼ cp. Honeydew Melon (Diced)
	¼ cp. Cantaloupe Melon (Diced)

30% Fat:	1 tb. "Lite" Mayonnaise

Method:
1) Combine the chili sauce, mayonnaise, garlic, and herbs to make dressing.

Serving:
1) Place lettuce in a bowl and top with crabmeat, melon, and peppers.
2) Pour the dressing over the salad.

Lunch Alternate: Turkey Salad with Melon and Herbed Mayonnaise
1) Omit the crabmeat and replace with deli turkey.

Nutrition Facts	
1 Serving	
Amount Per Serving	
Calories	286.6
Total Fat	8.5 g
Saturated Fat	0.9 g
Polyunsaturated Fat	0.2 g
Monounsaturated Fat	0.0 g
Cholesterol	155.3 mg
Sodium	1,162.3 mg
Potassium	614.0 mg
Total Carbohydrate	28.5 g
Dietary Fiber	4.6 g
Sugars	15.9 g
Protein	28.0 g
Vitamin A	190.7 %
Vitamin B-12	0.0 %
Vitamin B-6	21.0 %
Vitamin C	271.9 %
Vitamin D	0.0 %
Vitamin E	10.7 %
Calcium	11.9 %
Copper	4.1 %
Folate	10.8 %
Iron	18.4 %
Magnesium	6.7 %
Manganese	6.9 %
Niacin	8.4 %
Pantothenic Acid	6.4 %
Phosphorus	5.9 %
Riboflavin	6.1 %
Selenium	1.5 %
Thiamin	7.3 %
Zinc	3.1 %

Day 6

Snack

Toasted Chevre Cheese with Table Grapes

Yield: 1 Serving

30% Protein: 1½ oz. Slice Chevre (Creamy Goat Cheese)

40% Carbohydrate: 1 tsp. Seasoned Breadcrumbs (Pan Toasted)
                      ¼ cp. Seedless Red Grapes
                      ¼ cp. Red Cabbage (Shredded)

30% Fat: 1 tsp. Chopped Walnuts

Method:
1) Press breadcrumbs onto cheese.

Serving:
1) On a plate place a bed of cabbage with the breaded cheese on top.
2) Garnish with the walnuts and surround with grapes.

Snack Alternate: Buffalo Mozzarella with Table Grapes
1) Omit the Chevre and replace with fresh Mozzarella.

Nutrition Facts	
1 Serving	
Amount Per Serving	
Calories	186.6
Total Fat	12.0 g
Saturated Fat	6.6 g
Polyunsaturated Fat	2.2 g
Monounsaturated Fat	2.4 g
Cholesterol	19.6 mg
Sodium	288.0 mg
Potassium	141.1 mg
Total Carbohydrate	14.5 g
Dietary Fiber	1.5 g
Sugars	5.5 g
Protein	10.0 g
Vitamin A	14.6 %
Vitamin B-12	1.4 %
Vitamin B-6	11.4 %
Vitamin C	28.7 %
Vitamin D	0.0 %
Vitamin E	3.0 %
Calcium	9.0 %
Copper	21.2 %
Folate	5.7 %
Iron	8.6 %
Magnesium	5.4 %
Manganese	15.5 %
Niacin	4.5 %
Pantothenic Acid	4.0 %
Phosphorus	14.6 %
Riboflavin	13.8 %
Selenium	4.8 %
Thiamin	10.7 %
Zinc	4.5 %

Day 6

Dinner

Stuffed Bell Peppers with Garbanzo Beans and Sun-dried Tomato Salad

Yield: 1 Serving

30% Protein:	4 oz. Beef sirloin 93% Lean (Ground)
	½ oz. Egg Substitute

40% Carbohydrate:	½ cp. Chickpeas (canned)
	¼ cp. Red onion (chopped)
	1 tb. Sun-dried tomatoes (chopped)
	1 tb. Balsamic vinegar
	1 ea. Sm. Bell Pepper (halved)
	1 tbs. Bread Crumbs (seasoned)
	½ cp. Tomato Sauce (prepared or canned)
	1 tsp. Basil (chopped)

30% Fat:	2 tsp. Olive oil

Method:
1) Combine the beef, egg, and breadcrumbs then stuff each half with mixture. Top with tomato sauce and bake in a casserole dish at 350 degrees until meat is done and pepper halves are tender.
2) Combine the chickpeas, red onion, olive oil, basil, sun-dried tomato, and balsamic vinegar to make salad.

Serving: Place pepper halves on a plate and surround with chickpea salad.

Dinner Alternate: Turkey Stuffed Bell Peppers with Garbanzo Beans and Sun-dried Tomato Salad
1) Omit. Beef and replace with 4 oz. ground turkey

Nutrition Facts	
1 Serving	
Amount Per Serving	
Calories	475.1
Total Fat	19.1 g
Saturated Fat	4.6 g
Polyunsaturated Fat	1.7 g
Monounsaturated Fat	7.0 g
Cholesterol	65.3 mg
Sodium	998.4 mg
Potassium	895.1 mg
Total Carbohydrate	44.8 g
Dietary Fiber	8.2 g
Sugars	6.1 g
Protein	33.8 g
Vitamin A	145.7 %
Vitamin B-12	5.1 %
Vitamin B-6	37.6 %
Vitamin C	397.1 %
Vitamin D	2.5 %
Vitamin E	15.2 %
Calcium	8.4 %
Copper	20.6 %
Folate	29.0 %
Iron	20.5 %
Magnesium	16.0 %
Manganese	44.3 %
Niacin	14.2 %
Pantothenic Acid	9.9 %
Phosphorus	17.4 %
Riboflavin	24.0 %
Selenium	14.5 %
Thiamin	22.4 %
Zinc	9.8 %

Day 6

Snack (Dessert)

Butterscotch Chip Cookies

Yield: 2 Serving

30% Protein:	2 tb. Liquid Egg Substitute or 1 ea. Whole Egg (Cholesterol)
	1 tb. Soy Protein Powder
40% Carbohydrate:	¼ cp. Whole Grain Flour
	1 tb. Soy Flour
	2 tb. Brown Sugar (Light)
	½ tsp. Vanilla Extract
	2 tb. Butterscotch Chips
	Pinch Baking Soda
30% Fat:	2 tb. Soy Butter or Unsalted/Sweet Butter

Method:
1) In a mixer cream together the soy butter and brown sugar.
2) Beat in the eggs and vanilla extract.
3) Add the dry ingredients and the chips.
4) Use a scoop, flatten and bake at 300 degrees until browned and set

Serving:
1 Two cookies.

Snack Alternate: Chocolate Chip Cookies
1) Omit the butterscotch chips and replace with chocolate chips.

Nutrition Facts	
2 Servings	
Amount Per Serving	
Calories	127.4
Total Fat	6.6 g
Saturated Fat	2.1 g
Polyunsaturated Fat	2.1 g
Monounsaturated Fat	2.1 g
Cholesterol	0.7 mg
Sodium	247.3 mg
Potassium	74.4 mg
Total Carbohydrate	14.7 g
Dietary Fiber	0.7 g
Sugars	11.2 g
Protein	3.3 g
Vitamin A	1.2 %
Vitamin B-12	1.3 %
Vitamin B-6	1.2 %
Vitamin C	0.0 %
Vitamin D	0.7 %
Vitamin E	0.5 %
Calcium	2.0 %
Copper	3.8 %
Folate	4.7 %
Iron	3.8 %
Magnesium	3.5 %
Manganese	15.1 %
Niacin	1.4 %
Pantothenic Acid	1.1 %
Phosphorus	5.0 %
Riboflavin	4.7 %
Selenium	5.1 %
Thiamin	2.6 %
Zinc	2.1 %

Day 6

Scrambled Eggs on English Muffin with Black Forest Ham and Sautéed Spinach and Choron Sauce

Black forest ham is a German smoked boneless ham with a blackened skin. Traditionally, the color came from smoking the ham with resin-containing woods, but is also achieved by dipping it in a caramel solution. **English muffin** is a thin, round bread made with yeast dough and baked on a griddle.
Carb: English muffin, Spinach, Hollandaise Sauce, Tomato Paste
Protein: Egg Substitute, Black Forrest Ham, Skim Milk
Fat: Olive Oil

Beef Stuffed Bell Peppers with Garbanzo Beans and Sundried Tomato Salad

Garbanzo beans, also known as chickpea, is a somewhat spherical, irregular-shaped, pea-like seed of a plant. It has a firm texture and a nutty flavor. It is high in fiber, protein and a very good source of foliate and manganese.
Carb: Chickpeas, Onion, Tomatoes, Peppers, Breadcrumbs
Protein: Beef, Egg
Fat: Olive Oil

Toasted Chevre Cheese with Table Grapes

Chevre is French for goat. It is any French goat's milk cheese, usually pure white with a tart flavor with the textures ranging from soft, moist, and creamy to dry, firm, and crumbly.
Carb: Breadcrumbs, Grapes, Red Cabbage
Protein: Chevre
Fat: Walnut Oil, Walnuts

Seafood Salad and Herbed Mayonnaise

Honeydew is a slightly ovoid, large muskmelon. It has a smooth, creamy-yellow rind with a pale green, juicy flesh and a sweet flavor. This food is low in sodium and very low in saturated fat and cholesterol. It is also a good source of vitamin B6 and C, foliate and potassium.
Carb: Melons
Protein: Seafood
Fat: Mayonnaise

Day 6

Ingredient List

Dairy/Eggs:
6 oz. Egg Substitute
4 oz. Non-Fat Half & Half
2 oz. Chevre Goat Cheese
1 oz. Soy Butter or Unsalted/Sweet Butter

Dry Goods:
1 ea. Whole Wheat English Muffin
¼ oz. Tomato Paste
¼ oz. Canola Oil
½ oz. Olive Oil
¼ oz. Chili Sauce
¼ oz. Dried Tarragon, Basil, Garlic Powder
1 oz. Lite Mayonnaise
2 oz. Seasoned Bread Crumbs
½ oz. Walnuts
4 oz. Canned Chick Peas
1 oz. Balsamic Vinegar
4 oz. Prepared Tomato Sauce
2 oz. Whole Grain Flour
½ oz. Soy Flour
1 oz. Brown Sugar
¼ oz. Vanilla Extract
¼ oz. Baking Soda
½ oz. Soy Protein Powder
1 oz. Butter Scotch Chips

Meats:
2 oz. Ham
4 oz. Canned Pulled Blue Claw Crab
4 oz. Ground Beef

Produce:
2 ea. Hd. Spinach
4 cps. Mixed Salad Greens
2 ea. Sm. Green Peppers
1 ea. Sm. Red Pepper
½ ea. Honeydew, Cantaloupe Melon
2 oz. Seedless Grapes
2 oz. Shredded Red Cabbage
1 ea. Red Onion
1 oz. Sun Dried Tomatoes
1 ea. Sprig Basil

Day 7

Breakfast

Orange Cranberry "Power Muffin" with Orange Soy Butter and Glass of Milk

Yield: 1 Serving

30% Protein:	1 tb. Soy Protein Powder
	2 tb. Liquid Egg Substitute
	8 oz. Skim Milk
	2 tb. Non Fat Half & Half
40% Carbohydrate:	¼ cp. Dry Whole Bran Muffin Mix
	1 tsp. Orange Juice Concentrate
	1 tsp. Cranraisins
30% Fat:	1 tsp. Canola oil
	1 tb. Soy Butter or Unsalted/Sweet Butter

Suggestion: Double or triple the recipe, bake a day in advance, and reserve.

Method:
1) Combine all ingredients, pour into a jumbo muffin pan, and bake at 350 degrees for twenty minutes or until set.
2) Combine the concentrate with the butter to make the spread.

Serving: Cut the muffin in half and microwave for twenty seconds to slightly reheat then spread the butter and pour a glass of skim milk to accompany.

Breakfast Alternate: Scrambled Egg Whites with Cheddar Cheese and Seven Grain Toast

Yield: 1 Serving

30% Protein:	4 oz. Egg Whites
	½ oz. Shredded Cheddar Cheese
40% Carbohydrate:	2 ea. Slice Whole Grain Toast
30% Fat:	1 tsp. Canola Oil
	1 tsp. Soy Butter

1) Scramble egg whites in the oil and top with cheese.
2) Place soy butter on the side.

Serving: With toast

Nutrition Facts	
1 Serving	
Amount Per Serving	
Calories	379.5
Total Fat	17.8 g
Saturated Fat	4.5 g
Polyunsaturated Fat	5.1 g
Monounsaturated Fat	7.0 g
Cholesterol	2.7 mg
Sodium	538.9 mg
Potassium	490.7 mg
Total Carbohydrate	46.2 g
Dietary Fiber	0.4 g
Sugars	31.7 g
Protein	8.2 g
Vitamin A	9.0 %
Vitamin B-12	18.1 %
Vitamin B-6	7.4 %
Vitamin C	8.9 %
Vitamin D	9.0 %
Vitamin E	6.9 %
Calcium	16.7 %
Copper	1.3 %
Folate	9.0 %
Iron	3.9 %
Magnesium	8.6 %
Manganese	0.4 %
Niacin	1.5 %
Pantothenic Acid	14.8 %
Phosphorus	20.8 %
Riboflavin	48.0 %
Selenium	18.4 %
Thiamin	11.7 %
Zinc	4.9 %

Day 7

Lunch

Monterey Steak Salad Platter with Chili Roasted Corn Cob

Yield: 1 Serving

30% Protein:	4 oz. Sirloin Steak (Grass fed is best, less fat)
40% Carbohydrate:	4 cps. Mesclun Salad Greens
	1 ea. Md. Corn Cob
	¼ cp. Grape Tomatoes
	¼ cp. Red Onion (Slivered)
	½ tsp. Fresh Oregano
	2 tb. Lemon Juice
	½ tsp. Chili Powder
30% Fat:	2 tsp. Olive Oil

Method:
1) Combine the chili powder with ½ tsp. oil and roll corn in it. Roast at 425 degrees, reserve.
2) Season steak and grill (MR), cool, slice, and reserve.
3) Combine the oregano with the lemon juice and remaining oil to make dressing.

Serving:
1) Cut corn into wheels and place over the greens, top with sliced steak and surrounded by tomatoes and onions.
2) Pour the dressing over the steak and greens.

Lunch Alternate: Monterey Chicken Salad with Chili Roasted Corn Cob
1) Omit the beef and replace with 4 oz. chicken breast.

Nutrition Facts	
1 Serving	
Amount Per Serving	
Calories	443.3
Total Fat	19.3 g
Saturated Fat	4.9 g
Polyunsaturated Fat	1.7 g
Monounsaturated Fat	10.8 g
Cholesterol	100.9 mg
Sodium	120.3 mg
Potassium	773.0 mg
Total Carbohydrate	29.8 g
Dietary Fiber	5.5 g
Sugars	8.8 g
Protein	39.5 g
Vitamin A	137.2 %
Vitamin B-12	53.8 %
Vitamin B-6	33.1 %
Vitamin C	92.9 %
Vitamin D	0.0 %
Vitamin E	7.1 %
Calcium	7.8 %
Copper	12.3 %
Folate	14.5 %
Iron	36.2 %
Magnesium	18.1 %
Manganese	12.8 %
Niacin	31.6 %
Pantothenic Acid	10.5 %
Phosphorus	36.1 %
Riboflavin	23.2 %
Selenium	54.4 %
Thiamin	21.5 %
Zinc	52.5 %

Day 7

Snack

"Black Strap" BBQ Shrimp with Georgia Peach Compote

Yield: 1 Serving

30% Protein:	3 ea. Peeled Shrimp (16/20 per lb.)
40% Carbohydrate:	1 ea. Whole Peach (Pitted)
	1 tb. BBQ Sauce
	1 tb. Molasses
	½ tsp. Brown Sugar
	1 tb. Onion (Minced)
30% Fat:	1 tsp. Canola Oil

Method:
1) Marinate shrimp in molasses and BBQ sauce then grill.
2) In a sauce pot sauté the onions in the oil.
3) Add the peach and sugar with ½ cp. water, cook until thickened into compote.

Serving:
1) Place the compote on a plate and surround with the shrimp.

Snack Alternate: "Black Strap" Chicken Nuggets with Georgia Peach Compote
1) Omit the shrimp and replace with 2 oz. of chicken thigh meat.

Nutrition Facts	
1 Serving	
Amount Per Serving	
Calories	208.3
Total Fat	5.5 g
Saturated Fat	0.6 g
Polyunsaturated Fat	1.7 g
Monounsaturated Fat	2.8 g
Cholesterol	165.8 mg
Sodium	256.2 mg
Potassium	575.3 mg
Total Carbohydrate	21.6 g
Dietary Fiber	1.8 g
Sugars	5.1 g
Protein	18.4 g
Vitamin A	12.2 %
Vitamin B-12	21.1 %
Vitamin B-6	10.2 %
Vitamin C	12.9 %
Vitamin D	0.0 %
Vitamin E	9.7 %
Calcium	12.5 %
Copper	21.4 %
Folate	1.9 %
Iron	24.9 %
Magnesium	14.2 %
Manganese	17.0 %
Niacin	15.5 %
Pantothenic Acid	5.2 %
Phosphorus	13.3 %
Riboflavin	4.0 %
Selenium	51.2 %
Thiamin	3.2 %
Zinc	10.4 %

Day 7

Dinner

Pepper Jack Cheese and Red Pepper Roasted Chicken Breast on Fennel Bed

Yield: 1 Serving

		Nutrition Facts
30% Protein:	4 oz. Chicken Breast (Pounded)	
	1 oz. Pepper Jack Cheese	

30% Protein:
- 4 oz. Chicken Breast (Pounded)
- 1 oz. Pepper Jack Cheese

40% Carbohydrate:
- 3 cps. Fennel Bulb (Shredded)
- ½ cp. Red Bliss Potato (Diced)
- ½ cp. Chicken Broth
- 1 ea. Md. Red Pepper (Roasted/Peeled)
- ½ Tb. Cornstarch's

30% Fat:
- 2 tb. Non-Fat Half and Half

Nutrition Facts

1 Serving
Amount Per Serving

Calories	391.5
Total Fat	4.8 g
Saturated Fat	2.1 g
Polyunsaturated Fat	0.7 g
Monounsaturated Fat	1.4 g
Cholesterol	74.4 mg
Sodium	674.1 mg
Potassium	2,083.8 mg
Total Carbohydrate	49.7 g
Dietary Fiber	12.2 g
Sugars	2.3 g
Protein	39.9 g
Vitamin A	144.7 %
Vitamin B-12	14.2 %
Vitamin B-6	65.3 %
Vitamin C	456.3 %
Vitamin D	0.0 %
Vitamin E	5.1 %
Calcium	31.1 %
Copper	22.7 %
Folate	30.0 %
Iron	23.7 %
Magnesium	29.0 %
Manganese	45.2 %
Niacin	86.0 %
Pantothenic Acid	20.7 %
Phosphorus	63.9 %
Riboflavin	24.2 %
Selenium	41.7 %
Thiamin	17.9 %
Zinc	17.8 %

Method:
1) Roast the chicken breast in a 350 degree oven until golden brown along with the pepper, reserve.
3) In the broth separately poach the potatoes and fennel, remove, and reserve the broth.
4) Make a sauce by pureeing the pepper in a blender and adding it to the chicken broth with 1 tb. Half & Half.
5) Make slurry by combining the remaining 1 tb. Half & Half with the cornstarch.
6) In a sauce pot bring the broth to a boil and add the slurry to thicken into a sauce.

Serving:
1) Place the fennel and potatoes on a plate with the chicken on top.
2) Pour the sauce over the chicken.
3) Top with shredded cheese.

Dinner Alternate: Poached Chicken Breast with Fennel and Potatoes
1) Omit the cheese and poach chicken breast.

Day 7

Snack (Dessert)
Espresso Cupcakes

Yield: 1 Serving

30% Protein:	1 tb. Egg Substitute
	1 tsp. Soy Protein Powder
	2 tb. Buttermilk

40% Carbohydrate:	4 tb. Whole Grain Cake Flour
	1 tb. Soy Flour
	Pinch Baking Soda
	½ tsp. Instant Coffee (Decaffeinated)
	1 tb. Brown Sugar
	¼ tsp. Vanilla Extract

30% Fat:	1 tsp. Canola Oil

Suggestion: Double or triple the recipe, bake a day in advance, and reserve.

Method:
1) Whisk together the egg substitute and oil until foamy.
2) Add and whisk until smooth the brown sugar.
3) Add the buttermilk and vanilla.
4) Add the dry ingredients and whisk further until smooth.
5) Scoop the batter into a cupcake liner and place in a muffin tin. Bake at 300 degrees for twenty-five minutes until set in the middle.

Serving:
1) As is.

Snack Alternate: Cocoa Cupcakes
1) Omit the instant espresso and replace with cocoa powder.

Nutrition Facts	
1 Serving	
Amount Per Serving	
Calories	105.7
Total Fat	5.5 g
Saturated Fat	0.5 g
Polyunsaturated Fat	1.7 g
Monounsaturated Fat	3.0 g
Cholesterol	0.9 mg
Sodium	355.6 mg
Potassium	177.2 mg
Total Carbohydrate	9.5 g
Dietary Fiber	0.5 g
Sugars	6.8 g
Protein	6.1 g
Vitamin A	4.3 %
Vitamin B-12	11.3 %
Vitamin B-6	7.4 %
Vitamin C	0.2 %
Vitamin D	2.3 %
Vitamin E	6.0 %
Calcium	4.0 %
Copper	9.0 %
Folate	5.6 %
Iron	6.8 %
Magnesium	3.0 %
Manganese	8.1 %
Niacin	9.2 %
Pantothenic Acid	6.5 %
Phosphorus	8.1 %
Riboflavin	13.1 %
Selenium	7.8 %
Thiamin	10.8 %
Zinc	19.5 %

Day 7

Orange Cranberry Power Muffin

A medium-sized *orange* contains over 110 percent of the daily value of vitamin C. When choosing oranges, make sure they are firm and heavy. Store either at room temperature or in the refrigerator for about two weeks. *Did you know*, when fresh, good cranberries bounce and bad ones don't?

They are a good source of dietary fiber, manganese, vitamin C, E, and K.

Carb: Cake Flour, White Rice Flour, Orange, Cranberry Raisins
Protein: Protein Powder, Eggs
Fat: Oil

Monterey Steak Platter with Chili Roasted Corn on the Cob

Radicchio is a variety of chicory native to Italy. They are purple and white cup-shaped leaves that have a bitter flavor and can be used in salads, as garnish or cooked like a vegetable.

Carb: Radicchio, Corn, Onion, Tomatoes
Protein: Steak
Fat: Olive Oil

BBQ Shrimp with Georgia Peach Compote

Peaches are stone fruits native to China that are available as clingstone, in which the flesh "clings" to the pit and freestone, in which the flesh is easily pulled away from the pit. Peaches are a good source of dietary fiber, vitamins A and C, niacin, and potassium. *Did you know* nectarines are just peaches without the fuzz?

Carb: Peach, Onions
Protein: Shrimp
Fat: Olive Oil

Pepper Jack Cheese and Red Pepper with Chicken Breast

Fresh *peppers* are found in a wide range of colors—green, red, and yellow, orange, purple or white, as well as shapes. Peppers are excellent sources of Vitamins A and C. Keep them in the vegetable crisper compartment in the fridge for up to a week.

Carb: Potatoes, Chicken Broth, Vegetables, Red Pepper
Protein: Chicken, Cheese
Fat: Cream

Day 7

Ingredient List

Dairy/Eggs
8 oz. Skim Milk
1 oz. Egg Substitute
2 oz. Non-fat Half & Half
½ oz. Soy Butter
1 oz. Pepper Jack Cheese
1 oz. Buttermilk
¼ oz. Soy Butter or Unsalted/Sweet Butter

Dry Goods:
2 oz. Dry Whole Bran Muffin Mix
1 oz. Canola Oil
¼ oz. Fz. Orange Concentrate
¼ oz. Cranraisins
1 oz. Lemon Juice
¼ oz. Chili Powder
½ oz. Olive Oil
½ oz. Molasses
¼ oz. Granulated Sugar (Fructose Preferred)
½ oz. BBQ Sauce
4 oz. Chicken Broth
½ oz. Cornstarch
2 oz. Whole Grain Flour
½ oz. Soy Flour
¼ oz. Baking Soda
1 oz. Brown Sugar
¼ oz. Vanilla Extract
¼ oz. Instant decaffeinated Coffee

Seafood/Meats:
4 oz. Beef Sirloin Steak
3 ea. Shrimp Peeled/Deveined 16/20 per lb.
4 oz. Chicken Breast Skinless/Boneless

Produce:
1 ea. Sm. Sugar Banana
2 ea. Bulbs Fennel
1 ea. Red Onion
½ ea. Pineapple
1 ea. Red Pepper
1 ea. Sm. Zucchini, Yellow Squash
1 ea. Spaghetti Squash
2 ea. Plum Tomatoes
1 ea. Sprig Basil

Footnote

Due to packaging purposes, the amounts for each day's ingredients to be purchased are usually in excess of daily use. I have combined all **seven days** to make a complete list convenient for your one time shopping experience, yet I am sure that you probably already have some product in your pantry. Please follow along with each day's individual ingredient list, as you prepare your meals. It is wise to check off ingredients from the 7-day shopping list. Or if you wish you may shop accordingly to each daily ingredient list, but do so at least one day in advance.

Some other suggestions are not only to set aside one shopping day, but also to set aside a **baking day,** completing all seven days of desserts so as to have your "dessert snack" ready to be enjoyed without interruption.

I want you to have fun with this program, become educated in portion control and how to make a better food choice; by sticking with your new diet program, you'll be on your way to better health and noticeable weight loss.

Remember, making a better choice in diet and exercise is not only the right choice; it's the only way to a healthy lifestyle. So take your time and read through the recipes and ingredient lists. You're the chef who's preparing healthy and balanced meals for a full week, so enjoy it.

So what are you waiting for? Get cooking!

Days 1-7

Complete Weeks Shopping List

Dairy/Eggs:
12 oz. Non/Low-Fat Cottage Cheese
4 oz. Non/Low-Fat Cream Cheese
1 qt. Skim Milk
1 pt. Egg Substitute
½ lb. Soy Butter or Unsalted/Sweet Butter
½ pt. Buttermilk
½ lb. Skim Mozzarella
½ dz. Whole Eggs
¼ lb. Pepper Jack Cheese
4 oz. Plain Yogurt (Greek Preferred)
½ pt. Non/Low Fat Half & Half
½ pt. Liquid Egg Whites
2 oz. Fresh Mozzarella (Bocconcini) Balls
2 oz. Crumbled Blue Cheese
¼ lb. Colby or Monterey Jack Cheese
2 oz. Skim Ricotta

Dry Goods:
1 pkg. Fz. Crepe Shells
1 sm. Fz. Orange Juice Concentrate
1 sm. Jar Molasses
4 oz. Soy Protein Powder
2 oz. Vanilla Whey Protein Powder
1 lb. Brown Sugar
1 lb. Granulated Sugar (Fructose Preferred)
2 oz. Cocoa Powder
1 sm. Box Bran Muffin Mix
½ lb. Soy Flour
½ lb. Whole Grain Flour
½ lb. Rolled Oats or Oat flour
1 sm. Box Cornstarch
1 tin. Baking Powder
1 sm. Baking Soda
1 sm. Bottle Vanilla Extract
4 oz. Bag White or Dark Chocolate Chips
2 oz. Bag Butterscotch Chips
1 sm. Ground Cinnamon Powder

1 sm. Cajun Spice Powder
1 sm. Ginger Powder
1 sm. Dry Jerk Seasoning
1 sm. Ground Nutmeg
1 sm. Garlic Powder
1 sm. Dry Tarragon
1 sm. Dry Basil
1 sm. Chili Powder
1 sm. Can Prepared Tomato Sauce
1 sm. Can Plum Tomatoes
1 sm. Can Tomato Paste
1 sm. Can Chickpeas
1 sm. Bottle Cider Vinegar
1 sm. Bottle Raspberry Vinegar
1 sm. Bottle Balsamic Vinegar
1 sm. Box Brown Rice
1 sm. Bottle Lemon Juice
1 sm. Jar Decaffeinated Instant Coffee
1 sm. Bottle BBQ Sauce
1 pt. Canola Oil
1 pt. Olive Oil
1 sm. Bottle Honey
1 sm. Box Cornbread Mix
1 sm. Box Dry Polenta
1 sm. Box Seasoned Bread Crumbs
½ lb. Whole Grain Flour
1 sm. Box Buttermilk Pancake Mix
1 ea. Whole Grain Bread Roll
1 ea. Whole Wheat or Pumpernickel Bagel
1 ea. Whole Wheat English Muffin
½ lb. Whole Wheat Linguini Pasta
1 pkg. 6" Whole Wheat or Low Carb Tortilla
1 sm. Jar "Lite" Mayonnaise
½ pt. Beef Broth
½ pt. Chicken Broth
1 sm. Bottle "Diet" Maple Syrup
1 sm. Box Dark Raisins
1 sm. Box Cranraisins

¼ lb. Graham Cracker Crumbs
1 sm. Jar Apricot Preserves
1 sm. Can Pumpkin
1 sm. Jar Capers
1 sm. Bottle Kraft Catalina Dressing
1 sm. Can Artichoke Hearts
1 oz. ea. Walnuts, Macadamia Nuts, Almonds

Seafood/Meats:
9 ea. 1 oz. Shrimp 16/20 per lb. Peeled/Deveined
2 oz. Ahi Tuna
2 oz. Smoked Salmon
4 oz. Can Pulled Blue Claw Crabmeat
½ lb. Ground Beef
¼ lb. Deli Turkey
¼ lb. Veal Cutlet or stew Meat
¼ lb. Pork Canadian Bacon
¼ lb. Beef Top Round Cutlet
¼ lb. Boneless Pork Loin
¼ lb. Boneless/Skinless Chicken Thighs
¼ lb. Lamb Top Round or Stew Meat
¼ lb. Ground Beef
¼ lb. Deli Ham
¼ lb. Boneless/Skinless Chicken Breast
¼ lb. Beef Shell Steak

Produce:
1 pt. ea. Fresh Raspberries/ Strawberries
1 ea. sm. Cantaloupe, Honeydew Melon
1 ea. Lemon
1 sm. Head Napa Cabbage
2 ea. Spanish Onion
1 sm. Bunch Asparagus
2 ea lg. Bag Mixed Salad Greens
2 ea. Heads Collard Greens
1 ea. Carrot
1 ea. Sm. Garlic Blub
1 ea. Celery Stalk
1 ea. Dill, Cilantro
4 oz. Grape Tomatoes
6 ea. Plum Tomatoes
1 ea. Sm. Seedless Cucumber
1 ea. Stalk Scallion
2 ea. Red Onion
1 ea. Tomatillo (Green Tomato)
2 oz. Button Mushrooms
1 ea. Sm. Orange
1 ea. Sm. Yam
2 ea. Basil, Parsley Sprig
1 ea. Japanese Eggplant
2 ea. Red, Green, Yellow Peppers
1 ea. Sm. Sugar Banana
2 ea. Bulbs Fennel
½ ea. Pineapple
1 ea. Sm. Zucchini, Yellow Squash
1 ea. Spaghetti Squash
2 ea. Hd. Spinach
2 oz. Seedless Grapes
2 oz. Shredded Red Cabbage
1 oz. Sun Dried Tomatoes

MENU
Days 8-14

	Monday	Tuesday	Wednesday	Thursday	Friday	Saturday	Sunday
	Day 8	Day 9	Day10	Day11	Day12	Day13	Day14
Breakfast	Peaches and Ginger Cream with Heart Healthy Oatmeal Crepes	Blueberry and Hazelnut "Power" Oatmeal	"Mini" Croissant with Black Forrest Ham and Scrambled Eggs	Orange Ricotta "Protein" Pancakes with Mandarin-Honey Syrup	Non-Fat Sour Cream and Raisin Crepes	Crustless Southwestern Quiche with Fresh Berry Bowl	"Power" Oatmeal with Nuts and Apple-Cherry Compote
Lunch	Beef Tostada Salad w/ Corn Tortilla &Sour Cream Dressing	Turkey & Greek Salad Pocket Pita	Chicken Salad w/ Strawberry Peppercorn Vinaigrette	South Western Beef Stew w/ Jalapenos Chili's	Ham & Fruit Salad w/ Honey Mustard Vinaigrette	Sesame Crusted Fresh Tuna Fillet Salad w/ Ginger-Citrus Vinaigrette	Turkey Wrap w/ Herbed Mayo
Snack	Sweet Italian Sausage w/ Garbanzo Beans	Poached Salmon w/ Basil Mayo & Moroccan Couscous	Eggplant Italian Style	Fresh Melon Bowl w/ Minted Syrup & Vanilla Pistachio Yogurt	Roasted Beets w/ Creamy Chevre Cheese & Cranraisins	Roasted Root Vegetables & Ham Croquettes w/ Herbed Béchamel	Roasted Asparagus w/ Wisconsin Cheddar Fondue
Dinner	Almond Crusted Sea Bass w/ Basmati Rice	Maple Marinated Pork Chop w/ Roasted Vegetables	Vegetables & Bean Pilaf w/ Blackened Beef Rib Eye Steak	Pan Seared Sea Scallops w/ Rainbow Swiss Chard & Parmesan Gratin	Roasted Turkey w/ Acorn Squash Braised in Ginger-Orange Sauce	Chicken Tuscany in a White Wine Cream Sauce w/ Seedless Grapes	Grilled NY Shell Steak w/ Roasted Potatoes & Beef Steak Tomatoes w/ BBQ Sauce

Dessert	Pineapple Pistachio Crisp	White Chocolate Cream Cheese Mousse	Oatmeal & Date Cookie	Plum & Cherry Streusel Bar	Banana & Walnut Cupcakes	Fruit Cobbler	Pumpkin Mousse
Daily Calories	1,388.80	1,596.50	1,469.40	1,499.20	1,414.00	1,478.40	1,391.90

Day 8

Snack

Sweet Italian Sausage with Garbanzo Beans

Yield: 1 Serving

30% Protein:	½ ea. 4 oz. Link Italian Pork Sausage

40% Carbohydrate:	¼ cp. Chick Peas (Canned)
	1 tb. Onions (Diced)
	¼ tsp. Garlic (Minced)
	½ tsp. Tomato Paste
	½ tsp. Fresh Basil (Chopped)
	½ Tb. Balsamic Vinegar

30% Fat:	1 tsp. Olive Oil

Method:
1) In a skillet sauté the sausage in the oil. Remove and reserve.
2) Add the onion, garlic, tomato paste to the oil.
3) Place the chick peas in the skillet and add the vinegar and basil.

Serving:
1) Place the garbanzo beans on a plate with the sausage sliced on top.

Snack Alternate: Chicken Italian Sausage with Garbanzo Beans
1) Omit the pork and replace with chicken sausage.

Nutrition Facts	
1 Serving	
Amount Per Serving	
Calories	218.0
Total Fat	12.3 g
Saturated Fat	3.5 g
Polyunsaturated Fat	1.4 g
Monounsaturated Fat	5.7 g
Cholesterol	21.5 mg
Sodium	444.2 mg
Potassium	387.5 mg
Total Carbohydrate	19.3 g
Dietary Fiber	4.5 g
Sugars	3.6 g
Protein	9.0 g
Vitamin A	8.9 %
Vitamin B-12	4.3 %
Vitamin B-6	8.4 %
Vitamin C	13.1 %
Vitamin D	0.0 %
Vitamin E	7.7 %
Calcium	1.9 %
Copper	6.9 %
Folate	1.9 %
Iron	6.9 %
Magnesium	4.4 %
Manganese	6.5 %
Niacin	9.2 %
Pantothenic Acid	2.0 %
Phosphorus	6.9 %
Riboflavin	5.6 %
Selenium	12.5 %
Thiamin	12.2 %
Zinc	4.8 %

Day 8

Dinner

Almond Crusted Sea Bass with Basmati Rice

Yield: 1 Serving

30% Protein:	4 oz. Sea Bass Fillet (Boneless/Skinless)
40% Carbohydrate:	½ cp. White Basmati Rice (Steamed)
	¼ cp. Snow Peas
	2 cp. Bok Choy Cabbage (Chopped)
	¼ tsp. ea. Ginger and Garlic Powder
	1 tb. Hoisin Sauce
	1 tb. "Lite" Soy Sauce
	1 tb. Rice Wine Vinegar
30% Fat:	1 tb. Almonds (Sliced)
	1 tsp. Olive Oil

Method:
1) Brush the fish with the oil and press almonds onto fillet. Bake at 300 degrees until fish is tender and almonds are golden brown.
2) Steam cabbage and snow peas. Reserve.
3) Make sauce by combining Hoisin, soy, and vinegar with ginger and garlic powder.

Serving:
1) Place the rice with the steamed vegetables on a plate.
2) Lay fish fillet over and spoon on sauce.

Dinner Alternate: Almond Crusted Chicken Breast with Basmati Rice
1) Omit fish and replace with 4 oz. chicken breast.

Nutrition Facts	
1 Serving	
Amount Per Serving	
Calories	394.1
Total Fat	12.6 g
Saturated Fat	2.0 g
Polyunsaturated Fat	2.6 g
Monounsaturated Fat	6.4 g
Cholesterol	60.5 mg
Sodium	979.7 mg
Potassium	741.9 mg
Total Carbohydrate	36.1 g
Dietary Fiber	3.5 g
Sugars	3.0 g
Protein	34.6 g
Vitamin A	76.9 %
Vitamin B-12	5.7 %
Vitamin B-6	27.0 %
Vitamin C	40.6 %
Vitamin D	0.0 %
Vitamin E	12.0 %
Calcium	10.6 %
Copper	6.6 %
Folate	3.1 %
Iron	6.5 %
Magnesium	21.7 %
Manganese	13.9 %
Niacin	13.1 %
Pantothenic Acid	10.2 %
Phosphorus	32.2 %
Riboflavin	15.4 %
Selenium	76.6 %
Thiamin	11.0 %
Zinc	5.9 %

Day 8

Snack (Dessert)

Pineapple Pistachio Crisp

Yield: 1 Serving

30% Protein:	1 tb. Soy Protein Powder

40% Carbohydrate: 2 tb. Whole Grain Flour
1 tb Soy Flour
1 tb. Cornmeal
1 tb. Brown Sugar
¼ cp. Chopped Pineapple

30% Fat: 2 tsp. Pistachio Nuts (Shelled)
1 tb. Soy Butter

Method:
1) In a processor chop the pistachios.
2) In a mixer paddle all dry ingredients and nuts well with the soy butter.
3) Place the chopped pineapple in the bottom of a 3-inch bake-able tin or ceramic ramekin.
4) Sprinkle the pistachio mixture over the fruit.
5) Bake at 300 degrees until bubbly for twenty minutes.

Serving:
1) As is in the container.

Alternate Snack: Blueberry Pistachio Crisp
1) Omit the pineapple and replace with blueberries.

Nutrition Facts	
1 Serving	
Amount Per Serving	
Calories	118.7
Total Fat	8.5 g
Saturated Fat	2.5 g
Polyunsaturated Fat	2.6 g
Monounsaturated Fat	2.5 g
Cholesterol	0.0 mg
Sodium	92.4 mg
Potassium	105.7 mg
Total Carbohydrate	6.9 g
Dietary Fiber	0.7 g
Sugars	2.1 g
Protein	4.4 g
Vitamin A	1.8 %
Vitamin B-12	6.3 %
Vitamin B-6	6.1 %
Vitamin C	0.5 %
Vitamin D	0.0 %
Vitamin E	0.3 %
Calcium	1.4 %
Copper	7.8 %
Folate	2.9 %
Iron	5.6 %
Magnesium	2.8 %
Manganese	7.4 %
Niacin	8.3 %
Pantothenic Acid	3.9 %
Phosphorus	5.1 %
Riboflavin	3.5 %
Selenium	2.9 %
Thiamin	8.5 %
Zinc	16.3 %

Day 8

Peaches and Ginger Cream Crepes

Peaches are stone fruits native to China that are available as clingstone, in which the flesh "clings" to the pit and freestone, in which the flesh is easily pulled away from the pit. *Did you know* nectarines are just peaches without the fuzz?

Carb: Whole Wheat Flour, Oatmeal Flakes, Peaches, Honey
Protein: ricotta Cheese, Egg, Non-Fat Half & Half
Fat: Olive Oil

Almond Crusted Sea Bass with Black Beans and Rice

Black beans are a good source of cholesterol-lowering fiber. They have the highest source of antioxidants out of red, brown, yellow, and white beans. Rinse well before cooking, making sure there are no pebbles or withered beans. Soaking the beans before cooking helps retain texture as well as nutrients. One cup of dried black beans yields two cups of cooked beans.

Carb: Rice, Black Beans, Snow Peas, Bok Choy
Protein: Fish
Fat: Olive Oil, Almonds

DAY 8

Ingredient List

Dairy/Eggs:
4 oz. Skim Ricotta
2 oz. Non Fat Half and Half
1 oz. Egg Substitute
½ oz. Shredded Pepper Jack Cheese
½ oz. Non Fat Sour Cream
½ oz. Soy Butter or Unsalted/Sweet Butter

Dry Goods:
3 oz. Whole Grain Flour
2 oz. Rolled Oats
1 oz. Soy Flour
1 oz. Cornmeal
1 oz. Brown Sugar
1 oz. Honey
½ oz. Powdered Ginger, Garlic, Chili's
1 oz. Canola, Olive Oil
1 oz. Hoisin, "Lite" Soy Sauce
1 oz. ea. Rice Wine, Balsamic Vinegar
½ oz. Sliced Almonds, Pistachios
2 oz. Basmati Rice
2 oz. Canned Chick Peas
½ oz. Tomato Paste
4 oz. Beef Broth
1 oz. "Lite" Mayonnaise
1 ea. 6" Corn Tortilla

Seafood/Meats:
6 oz. Sea Bass Fillet (Boneless/Skinless)
4 oz. Beef Brisket
2 oz. Italian sweet Pork Sausage

Produce:
2 ea. Md. Peaches
16 oz. Bok Choy Cabbage
2 oz. Snow Peas
2 ea. Plum Tomatoes
2 cp. Mixed Green Salad
1 oz. Lemon, Lime Juice
2 oz. Scallions
1 oz. Sp. Onion
2 ea. Garlic Cloves
1 ea. Sprig Basil
2 oz. Pineapple

Day 9

Breakfast

Blueberry and Hazelnut "Power" Oatmeal

Yield: 1 Serving

30% Protein:	1 tb. Vanilla Whey or Soy Protein Powder
	1 cp. Skim Milk
40% Carbohydrate:	½ cp. Old Fashioned Oats or Irish Groats
	¼ cp. Frozen Blueberries
	1 tb. Honey
	¼ tsp. Ground Cinnamon
	¼ tsp. Vanilla Extract
	1 tb. Brown Sugar
30% Fat:	2 tsp. Chopped Hazelnuts

Method:
1) Bring the milk to a boil in a sauce pot and stir in the oats.
2) Reduce heat to a simmer and cook until oats are tender.
3) Remove from heat and stir in the sugar, blueberries, extract, and cinnamon.

Serving:
1) Place the oatmeal in a microwaveable container and top with the honey and hazelnuts.

Breakfast Alternate: Mango and Coconut "Power" Oatmeal
1) Replace the blueberries with mango.
2) Replace the hazelnuts with coconut.

Nutrition Facts	
1 Serving	
Amount Per Serving	
Calories	368.2
Total Fat	8.6 g
Saturated Fat	2.4 g
Polyunsaturated Fat	1.9 g
Monounsaturated Fat	4.9 g
Cholesterol	13.1 mg
Sodium	272.5 mg
Potassium	952.8 mg
Total Carbohydrate	72.6 g
Dietary Fiber	6.9 g
Sugars	43.5 g
Protein	14.1 g
Vitamin A	10.4 %
Vitamin B-12	23.8 %
Vitamin B-6	15.6 %
Vitamin C	4.4 %
Vitamin D	31.7 %
Vitamin E	11.1 %
Calcium	44.8 %
Copper	22.0 %
Folate	12.4 %
Iron	14.5 %
Magnesium	34.7 %
Manganese	124.9 %
Niacin	6.7 %
Pantothenic Acid	24.2 %
Phosphorus	60.6 %
Riboflavin	51.7 %
Selenium	17.9 %
Thiamin	33.0 %
Zinc	20.8 %

Day 9

Snack

Poached Salmon with Basil Mayonnaise and Moroccan Couscous

Yield: 1 Serving

30% Protein: 2 oz. Salmon Fillet (Boneless/Skinless)
 ½ oz. Plain Yogurt

40% Carbohydrate: ¼ cp. Dry Couscous
 ¼ tsp. Fresh Basil
 ¼ tsp. Fresh Parsley
 1 tb. Scallion (Chopped)
 ½ cp. Chicken Broth
 Pinch Saffron

30% Fat: 1 tb. "Lite" Mayonnaise

Method:
1) Poach (simmer) the salmon in the broth for five minutes or until you see white fat striations appear on the surface, reserve chilled.
2) In the poaching liquid after the salmon has been removed cook the couscous and saffron by simmering over low heat until done.
3) Combine the yogurt, mayonnaise with the herbs in a processor and puree to make dressing.

Serving:
1) Place the couscous in a non-microwaveable container with the salmon on top, garnish with the scallion.
2) Spoon on the dressing.

Snack Alternate: Poached Chicken Breast with Basil Mayonnaise and Moroccan Couscous
1) Omit the salmon and replace with 2 oz. chicken breast.

Nutrition Facts	
1 Serving	
Amount Per Serving	
Calories	234.2
Total Fat	11.5 g
Saturated Fat	2.4 g
Polyunsaturated Fat	1.9 g
Monounsaturated Fat	1.7 g
Cholesterol	47.2 mg
Sodium	549.5 mg
Potassium	446.3 mg
Total Carbohydrate	14.7 g
Dietary Fiber	0.7 g
Sugars	3.5 g
Protein	17.8 g
Vitamin A	5.0 %
Vitamin B-12	31.4 %
Vitamin B-6	27.6 %
Vitamin C	2.3 %
Vitamin D	0.0 %
Vitamin E	3.0 %
Calcium	6.5 %
Copper	9.5 %
Folate	5.8 %
Iron	5.5 %
Magnesium	6.7 %
Manganese	1.1 %
Niacin	28.9 %
Pantothenic Acid	12.6 %
Phosphorus	19.7 %
Riboflavin	20.1 %
Selenium	39.3 %
Thiamin	11.4 %
Zinc	4.9 %

Day 9

Dinner

Maple Marinated Pork Chop with Roasted Vegetable

Yield: 1 Serving

30% Protein: 6 oz. Pork Chop (Bone In)

40% Carbohydrate: ½ cp. Butternut Squash (Sm. Dice)
                      ¼ cp. Pineapple (Sm. Dice)
                      ¼ cp. 'Diet' Maple Syrup
                      ¼ cp. Zucchini (Sm. dice)
                      ¼ cp. Cherry Tomatoes

30% Fat: 2 tsp. Olive oil

Method:
1) Marinate pork chop in syrup and the oil. Place the squash in a roasting pan under the chop and then roast at 350 degrees until pork and squash are almost done.
2) When the pork and squash are almost finished, combine all remaining vegetables and pineapple. Add to the pan and continue to roast until all vegetables are tender.

Serving: Place the squash on a plate with the pork chop on top and surround with the rest of the cooked vegetables and fruit.

Dinner Alternate: Maple Marinated Chicken Thigh with Roasted Vegetable
1) Omit the pork chop and replace with 4 oz. chicken thigh (boneless/skinless).

Nutrition Facts	
1 Serving	
Amount Per Serving	
Calories	432.7
Total Fat	20.2 g
Saturated Fat	5.1 g
Polyunsaturated Fat	2.0 g
Monounsaturated Fat	11.4 g
Cholesterol	89.5 mg
Sodium	91.6 mg
Potassium	1,012.3 mg
Total Carbohydrate	30.4 g
Dietary Fiber	5.6 g
Sugars	5.1 g
Protein	34.8 g
Vitamin A	162.1 %
Vitamin B-12	11.0 %
Vitamin B-6	31.1 %
Vitamin C	66.1 %
Vitamin D	0.0 %
Vitamin E	6.1 %
Calcium	7.8 %
Copper	11.2 %
Folate	16.3 %
Iron	14.5 %
Magnesium	22.9 %
Manganese	19.6 %
Niacin	43.0 %
Pantothenic Acid	17.6 %
Phosphorus	35.9 %
Riboflavin	22.4 %
Selenium	71.4 %
Thiamin	84.8 %
Zinc	19.5 %

Day 9

Snack (Dessert)

White Chocolate Cream Cheese Mousse

Yield: 1 Serving

30% Protein:	4 tb. Low-Fat Cream Cheese
40% Carbohydrate:	1 tsp. Fruit Sugar (Fructose Preferred)
	¼ tsp. Vanilla Extract
	1 tb. White Chocolate
30% Fat:	2 tb. Half and Half

Method:
1) Melt the white chocolate in a microwave oven or in a double boiler on the stove top.
2) Whip together all ingredients in a bowl until completely aerated and light.

Serving:
1) Place the mousse in a sundae cup and garnish with white chocolate shavings, refrigerate.

Snack Alternate: Chocolate Cream Cheese Mousse
1) Omit the white chocolate and replace with 1 tsp. ea. cocoa powder and dark chocolate.
2) Omit the fructose and replace with brown sugar.

Nutrition Facts	
1 Serving	
Amount Per Serving	
Calories	195.6
Total Fat	16.3 g
Saturated Fat	10.2 g
Polyunsaturated Fat	0.6 g
Monounsaturated Fat	4.7 g
Cholesterol	45.7 mg
Sodium	135.8 mg
Potassium	96.4 mg
Total Carbohydrate	8.9 g
Dietary Fiber	0.3 g
Sugars	2.9 g
Protein	3.7 g
Vitamin A	11.7 %
Vitamin B-12	4.0 %
Vitamin B-6	1.4 %
Vitamin C	0.2 %
Vitamin D	0.0 %
Vitamin E	2.3 %
Calcium	5.5 %
Copper	1.9 %
Folate	1.5 %
Iron	3.2 %
Magnesium	2.1 %
Manganese	1.4 %
Niacin	0.4 %
Pantothenic Acid	1.8 %
Phosphorus	7.1 %
Riboflavin	7.2 %
Selenium	2.2 %
Thiamin	1.2 %
Zinc	2.6 %

Day 9

Blueberry and Hazelnut Power Oatmeal

Hazelnuts are high in Vitamin E, foliate, and B Vitamins. Hazelnuts are especially flavorful when roasted and used in desserts with berries and chocolate. *Did you know* over 95 percent of the U.S. commercial production is in Oregon's Willamette Valley?
Carb: Oats, Blueberries, Honey, Cinnamon, Brown Sugar
Protein: Vanilla Protein Powder, Skim Milk
Fat: Hazelnuts

Turkey Greek Salad Pocket Pita

Greek salad is a common component of a traditional Greek meal. A traditional Greek salad consists of sliced or chopped <u>tomatoes</u> with a few slices of <u>cucumber</u>, <u>red onion</u>, <u>feta</u> cheese, and Kalamata <u>olives</u>, seasoned with <u>salt</u>, <u>black pepper</u>, <u>oregano</u>, <u>basil</u> and dressed with <u>olive oil</u>.
Carb: Pita, Onions, Tomato
Protein: Turkey, Feta Cheese
Fat: Olive Oil

Poached Salmon with Basil Mayonnaise and
Moroccan Couscous

Salmon is part of a large family of anatropous fish found in the Northern Atlantic and Pacific Oceans. They have silver to gray skin, a pink-red flesh, a firm texture and a rich flavor. Salmon is high in protein, vitamin B12, and selenium (antioxidant). *Basil* is an herb and member of the mint family. It has soft, shiny light green leaves, small white flowers, and a strong, pungent, peppery flavor reminiscent of licorice and cloves.
Carb: Couscous, Scallion
Protein: Salmon, Yogurt
Fat: Diet Mayonnaise

Maple Marinated Pork Chop with Roasted Vegetable and Pineapple

Marinade is a seasoned liquid, usually containing an acid, herbs, and/or spices, in which raw foods are soaked or coated to absorb flavors and become tender before cooking or serving. *Pineapples* have significant amounts of vitamin C and manganese. Pineapple juice can be used as a marinade and as a tenderizer for meat. *Did you know* that one third of the world's pineapple comes from Hawaii?
Carb: Pineapple, Zucchini, Tomatoes, Corn
Protein: Pork
Fat: Olive Oil

Day 9

Ingredient List

Dairy/Eggs:
8 oz. Skim Milk
½ oz. Feta Cheese
½ oz. Plain Low-Fat Yogurt
1 oz. Low-Fat Cream Cheese
1 oz. Non-Fat Half and Half

Dry Goods:
1 oz. Vanilla Whey Protein Powder
4 oz. Rolled Oats
1 oz. Honey
¼ oz. Ground Cinnamon
¼ oz. Vanilla Extract
1 oz. Brown Sugar
½ oz. Hazelnuts
2 oz. Diet Maple Syrup
½ oz. Olive Oil
½ ea. Whole Wheat Pocket Pita
1 oz. Balsamic Vinegar
2 oz. Dry Couscous
4 oz. Chicken Broth
¼ oz. Saffron
1 oz. "Lite" Mayonnaise
½ oz. White Chocolate Chips or Dark
½ oz. Granulated Sugar (Fructose Preferred)

Meats/Seafood:
6 oz. Pork Chop (Bone In)
3 oz. Deli Turkey
3 oz. Salmon Fillet (Boneless/Skinless)

Produce:
½ ea. Sm. Butternut Squash
½ ea. Sm. Pineapple
½ ea. Sm. Zucchini
2 oz. Cherry Tomatoes
1 cp. Mixed Salad Greens
1 ea. Sm. Red Onion
1 ea. Tomato
1 ea. Sprig Dill, Parsley, Basil
1 ea. Scallion
2 oz. Blueberries

Day 10

Breakfast

Breakfast "Mini" Croissant with Black Forrest Ham and Scrambled Eggs

Yield: 1 Serving

30% Protein:	¼ cp. Egg Substitute
	1oz. Ham Slice

40% Carbohydrate:	1 ea.-1 oz. Croissant (Mini)
	½ cp. Honeydew Melon
	½ cp. Cantaloupe melon

30% Fat:	½ tb. Soy Butter or Unsalted/Sweet Butter
	1 tsp. Canola Oil

Method:
1) Scramble the egg substitute in the oil.
2) Grill the ham slices.

Serving:
1) Place the croissant on a plate with the ham and eggs.
2) Place the melon in a separate cup.
3) Spread the soy butter on the croissant.

Breakfast Alternate: Breakfast "Mini" Croissant with Scrambled Eggs
1) Omit the ham.

Nutrition Facts	
1 Serving	
Amount Per Serving	
Calories	372.8
Total Fat	19.0 g
Saturated Fat	6.4 g
Polyunsaturated Fat	3.8 g
Monounsaturated Fat	7.3 g
Cholesterol	46.3 mg
Sodium	1,227.9 mg
Potassium	842.3 mg
Total Carbohydrate	30.0 g
Dietary Fiber	2.2 g
Sugars	18.0 g
Protein	20.2 g
Vitamin A	21.0 %
Vitamin B-12	27.8 %
Vitamin B-6	25.6 %
Vitamin C	53.2 %
Vitamin D	10.0 %
Vitamin E	11.4 %
Calcium	4.5 %
Copper	6.0 %
Folate	30.2 %
Iron	13.3 %
Magnesium	9.4 %
Manganese	8.2 %
Niacin	20.9 %
Pantothenic Acid	17.8 %
Phosphorus	24.9 %
Riboflavin	62.7 %
Selenium	46.4 %
Thiamin	57.0 %
Zinc	13.8 %

Day 10

Lunch

Chicken Salad with Strawberry-Peppercorn Vinaigrette

Yield: 1 Serving

30% Protein:	4 oz. Poached Chicken Breast (Diced)

40% Carbohydrate: 4 cps. Mesclun Salad Greens
½ cp. Yellow/Red Grape Tomatoes
¼ cp. Enoki Mushrooms
½ cp. Steamed Chinese Black Rice
¼ cp. Fresh Strawberries (Sliced)
¼ tsp. Cracked Black Peppercorns
2 tb. Red Wine Vinegar
½ cp. Chicken Broth

30% Fat: 2 tsp. Canola Oil

Method:
1) Simmer the chicken in the broth until completely done and cooked throughout.
2) Combine the oil, vinegar, peppercorns with the strawberries to make vinaigrette.

Serving:
1) Place the salad greens in a bowl with the rice and chicken.
2) Surround with tomatoes and strawberries.
3) Pour the vinaigrette over the complete salad.
4) Garnish with the Enoki mushrooms.

Lunch alternate: Tuna Salad with Strawberry-Peppercorn Vinaigrette
1) Omit the chicken and replace with 4 oz. canned tuna.
2) Omit the mushroom garnish.

Nutrition Facts	
1 Serving	
Amount Per Serving	
Calories	403.4
Total Fat	11.4 g
Saturated Fat	1.2 g
Polyunsaturated Fat	3.4 g
Monounsaturated Fat	6.0 g
Cholesterol	65.7 mg
Sodium	100.7 mg
Potassium	498.8 mg
Total Carbohydrate	43.8 g
Dietary Fiber	5.1 g
Sugars	12.6 g
Protein	31.5 g
Vitamin A	131.6 %
Vitamin B-12	7.3 %
Vitamin B-6	40.0 %
Vitamin C	134.8 %
Vitamin D	3.3 %
Vitamin E	12.0 %
Calcium	7.4 %
Copper	12.0 %
Folate	5.2 %
Iron	21.3 %
Magnesium	22.0 %
Manganese	57.3 %
Niacin	75.5 %
Pantothenic Acid	15.3 %
Phosphorus	32.8 %
Riboflavin	13.1 %
Selenium	45.3 %
Thiamin	13.4 %
Zinc	11.2 %

Day 10

Snack

Eggplant Italiano

Yield: 1 Serving

30% Protein:	2 oz. Skim Mozzarella Cheese (Shredded)

40% Carbohydrate: 2 ea. ½" Slice Eggplant
¼ cp. Rolled Oats (toasted)
4 tb. Prepared Tomato Sauce
¼ tsp. Basil
¼ tsp. Oregano
¼ cp. Onions (chopped)
½ tsp. Garlic (minced)

30% Fat: ½ tsp. Olive Oil

Method:
1) Sauté the eggplant slices on both sides in the oil. Remove and reserve. Place the onions and garlic in the oil and combine with the tomato sauce and herbs.
2) Top the eggplant with toasted oats and cheese.
3) Bake 350 degrees in the tomato sauce for five minutes or until eggplant is tender and cheese melts.

Serving:
1) Place on a plate directly from oven.

Snack Alternate: Zucchini Squash Italiano
1) Omit the eggplant and replace with 1 ea. medium-sized squash sliced lengthwise.

Nutrition Facts	
1 Serving	
Amount Per Serving	
Calories	206.0
Total Fat	11.8 g
Saturated Fat	6.2 g
Polyunsaturated Fat	0.9 g
Monounsaturated Fat	4.5 g
Cholesterol	32.9 mg
Sodium	425.6 mg
Potassium	253.5 mg
Total Carbohydrate	14.4 g
Dietary Fiber	2.5 g
Sugars	1.3 g
Protein	15.3 g
Vitamin A	9.1 %
Vitamin B-12	7.7 %
Vitamin B-6	5.2 %
Vitamin C	4.2 %
Vitamin D	0.0 %
Vitamin E	5.2 %
Calcium	37.9 %
Copper	7.4 %
Folate	4.9 %
Iron	6.5 %
Magnesium	11.4 %
Manganese	37.7 %
Niacin	3.1 %
Pantothenic Acid	3.8 %
Phosphorus	34.8 %
Riboflavin	12.8 %
Selenium	11.8 %
Thiamin	9.0 %
Zinc	14.7 %

Day 10

Dinner

Vegetable and Bean Pilaf with Blackened Beef Rib Eye Steak

Yield: 1 Serving

30% Protein:	4 oz. Beef Rib Eye Steak (Grass Fed Preferred)
40% Carbohydrate:	½ cp. Beef Stock
	¼ cp. Onions (Chopped)
	¼ cp. Carrots (Diced)
	1 tb. Fresh Parsley (Minced)
	1 tb. Blackening Spices
	½ cp. Black Eye Peas (Canned)
	1 tb. Prepared Tomato Sauce
30% Fat:	2 tsp. Olive Oil

Method:
1) Dredge the steak in the blackening spices, in a skillet sear on both sides, and cook throughout, reserve.
2) In the same skillet heat the oil and add the onions, carrots and beans, toss to coat.
3) Add the beef stock and tomato sauce to the skillet and simmer until liquid reduces by half.

Serving:
1) Place the vegetables on a plate and put the steak on top, garnish with parsley.

Dinner Alternate: Vegetable and Bean Pilaf with Blackened Chicken Breast
1) Omit the beef and replace with 4 oz. chicken breast.

Nutrition Facts

1 Serving
Amount Per Serving

Calories	337.6
Total Fat	14.9 g
Saturated Fat	2.8 g
Polyunsaturated Fat	3.0 g
Monounsaturated Fat	7.7 g
Cholesterol	44.2 mg
Sodium	487.1 mg
Potassium	419.7 mg
Total Carbohydrate	21.0 g
Dietary Fiber	5.3 g
Sugars	4.5 g
Protein	28.1 g
Vitamin A	139.7 %
Vitamin B-12	57.9 %
Vitamin B-6	24.4 %
Vitamin C	9.7 %
Vitamin D	0.0 %
Vitamin E	10.1 %
Calcium	12.9 %
Copper	4.9 %
Folate	2.6 %
Iron	29.2 %
Magnesium	7.1 %
Manganese	1.4 %
Niacin	27.4 %
Pantothenic Acid	4.1 %
Phosphorus	23.3 %
Riboflavin	14.2 %
Selenium	17.4 %
Thiamin	8.5 %
Zinc	27.7 %

Day 10

Snack (Dessert)

Healthy Oatmeal Raisin Cookies

Yield: 2 Servings

30% Protein:	2 tb. Egg Substitute
	1 tb. Buttermilk
	1 tb. Soy Protein Powder

40% Carbohydrate:	¼ cp. Whole Grain Flour
	1 tb. Soy Flour
	Pinch Baking Soda
	¼ tsp. Vanilla Extract
	¼ tsp. Cinnamon Powder
	¼ cp. Rolled Oats
	1 tb. Dark Raisins
	1 tb. Brown Sugar

30% Fat:	2 tb. Soy Butter

Method:
1) Cream together with a paddle the soy butter, brown sugar, and cinnamon.
2) Beat in the egg substitute, vanilla, and buttermilk.
3) Add all dry ingredients and raisins, refrigerate until chilled,
4) Portion and flatten on a cookie sheet then bake at 300 degrees for twenty minutes or until golden brown.

Serving:
1) Place two cookies on a paper doily on a plate.

Snack Alternate: Oatmeal Date Cookies
1) Omit the raisins and replace with dates.

Nutrition Facts	
2 Servings	
Amount Per Serving	
Calories	86.5
Total Fat	5.0 g
Saturated Fat	1.1 g
Polyunsaturated Fat	1.7 g
Monounsaturated Fat	2.1 g
Cholesterol	0.2 mg
Sodium	85.7 mg
Potassium	118.5 mg
Total Carbohydrate	10.0 g
Dietary Fiber	1.1 g
Sugars	4.6 g
Protein	2.9 g
Vitamin A	1.8 %
Vitamin B-12	4.6 %
Vitamin B-6	3.7 %
Vitamin C	0.1 %
Vitamin D	0.7 %
Vitamin E	2.4 %
Calcium	1.6 %
Copper	6.1 %
Folate	3.5 %
Iron	4.6 %
Magnesium	4.2 %
Manganese	18.3 %
Niacin	4.3 %
Pantothenic Acid	3.6 %
Phosphorus	6.3 %
Riboflavin	6.2 %
Selenium	3.5 %
Thiamin	7.6 %
Zinc	9.6 %

Day 10

Sesame Flank Steak with Ginger-Carrot Rice

Sesame seeds lend a nutty flavor to foods, and they are also a great source of manganese, copper, calcium, and magnesium. If purchasing sesame seeds, make sure there is no presence of moisture, since they can go bad. Hulled seeds should be stored in an air-tight container in a dry place. *Ginger* adds a distinguishable, zesty flavor, usually found in Asian cuisines. Ginger is a popular herbal remedy for gastrointestinal relief, preventing motion sickness, as well as others.

Carb: Brown Rice, Carrots, Scallions
Protein: Steak
Fat: Sesame Seed Oil

Chicken Salad with Strawberry-Peppercorn Vinaigrette

Black Peppercorns are the berries of a vine plant native to tropical Asia. Black peppercorns are produced from the same plant, but are picked and processed differently. The berries are picked when green and simply dried whole in the sun. They have a warm, pungent flavor and aroma.

Carb: Mesclun Greens, Tomatoes, Mushrooms, Kiwi, Chinese Black Rice, Strawberries, Peppercorns, Vinegar
Protein: Chicken
Fat: Canola Oil

Breakfast Mini Croissant with Black Forrest Ham and Scrambled Eggs

Croissant is a rich, buttery, crescent-shaped roll made with flaky yeast dough. *Black Forrest Ham* is a German smoked boneless ham with a blackened skin. Traditionally, the color comes from smoking the ham with resin-containing woods.

Carb: Croissant, Honeydew, Cantaloupe
Protein: Egg Substitute, Ham
Fat: Soy Butter, Olive Oil

Eggplant Italiano

There are two types of *eggplants* commonly available: Asian and Western. Asian varieties are either round or long and thin, with skin colors ranging from creamy white to deep purple. Western eggplants, which are more common in the United States, tend to be shaped like a plump pear with shiny lavender to purple-black skin.

Carb: Eggplant, Oats, Tomato Sauce, Basil, Oregano, Onions, Garlic
Protein: Mozzarella Cheese
Fat: Olive Oil

DAY 10

Ingredient List

Dairy/Eggs:
3 oz. Egg Substitute
2 oz. Soy Butter or Unsalted/Sweet Butter
2 oz. Skim Mozzarella
1 oz. Buttermilk

Dry Goods:
1 ea. Mini Croissant
4 oz. Canned Black Eye Peas
2 oz. Prepared Tomato sauce
½ oz. Blackening Spices, Cracked Black Pepper
4 oz. Beef, Chicken Broth
½ oz. Olive, Canola Oil
2 oz. Black Chinese Rice
1 oz. Red Wine Vinegar
4 oz. Rolled Oats
½ oz. Soy Protein Powder
2 oz. Whole Grain Flour
½ oz. Soy Flour
¼ oz. Baking Soda
¼ oz. Vanilla Extract
¼ oz. Cinnamon Powder
½ oz. Brown Sugar
½ oz. Dark Raisins

Meats:
1 oz. Deli Ham
4 oz. Rib Eye Steak (Grass Fed Preferred)
4 oz. Chicken Breast

Produce:
½ ea. Sm. Cantaloupes, Honeydew Melon
1 ea. Sm. Sp. Onion
1 ea. Lg. Carrot
2 ea. Cloves Garlic
1 ea. Sprig Parsley, Basil, Oregano
4 cp. Mesclun Salad Greens
½ cp. Red, Yellow Grape Tomatoes
1 oz. Enoki Mushrooms
1 ea. Sm. Japanese Eggplant
2 oz. Strawberries

Day 11

Breakfast

Orange Ricotta "Protein" Pancakes with Mandarin-Honey Syrup

Yield: 1 Serving

30% Protein:	4 oz. Skim Ricotta Cheese
	2 tb. Skim Milk
	2 tb. Liquid Egg Substitute

40% Carbohydrate:	½ cp. Buttermilk Pancake Mix
	½ tsp. Orange Rind
	¼ tsp. Orange Extract
	¼ tsp. Granulated Sugar (Fructose Preferred)
	1 tb. Honey
	¼ cp. Mandarin Orange Segments (In Syrup)

| 30% Fat: | 2 tsp. Canola Oil |

Method:
1) Combine the cheese, milk, rind, extract, 1 tsp. oil, and sugar with the pancake mix.
2) Whisk the egg whites until frothy and fold into the batter.
3) In a skillet with 1 tsp. oil to coat the bottom, over low heat, spoon out the batter to make pancakes.
4) Combine 1 oz. of the reserved mandarin orange syrup and add the honey, reserve.

Serving:
1) Place the pancakes on a plate and garnish with orange segments.
2) Spoon on the honey mandarin syrup as needed.

Breakfast Alternate: Buttermilk "Protein" Pancakes with Honey
1) Omit the orange rind, extract, and syrup.

Nutrition Facts	
1 Serving	
Amount Per Serving	
Calories	347.4
Total Fat	19.0 g
Saturated Fat	0.8 g
Polyunsaturated Fat	3.3 g
Monounsaturated Fat	5.6 g
Cholesterol	60.6 mg
Sodium	267.7 mg
Potassium	353.1 mg
Total Carbohydrate	23.6 g
Dietary Fiber	0.8 g
Sugars	16.6 g
Protein	18.1 g
Vitamin A	37.9 %
Vitamin B-12	32.5 %
Vitamin B-6	5.1 %
Vitamin C	26.8 %
Vitamin D	17.5 %
Vitamin E	13.4 %
Calcium	40.1 %
Copper	1.9 %
Folate	17.1 %
Iron	8.5 %
Magnesium	5.3 %
Manganese	0.8 %
Niacin	1.5 %
Pantothenic Acid	10.1 %
Phosphorus	8.2 %
Riboflavin	58.6 %
Selenium	24.7 %
Thiamin	12.8 %
Zinc	6.8 %

Day 11

Lunch

Southwestern Beef Stew with Jalapeno Chili's

Yield: 1 Serving

30% Protein: 4 oz. Stew Meat (Cubed)

40% Carbohydrate: ¼ cp. Red Bliss Potatoes (Diced)
                     ¼ cp. Onions (Diced)
                     ½ cp. Plum Tomatoes (Canned)
                     ½ tsp. Garlic (Minced)
                     1 tsp. Jalapeno Peppers (Optional)
                     ¼ tsp. Ground Cumin
                     ¼ tsp. Chili Powder
                     ¼ tsp. Coriander
                     ¼ tsp. Fresh Cilantro (Minced)
                     ½ cp. Beef Broth

30% Fat: 2 tsp. Olive Oil

Method:
1) In a sauce pan sauté the garlic, onions, the beef in the oil, searing and browning the meat.
2) Add the tomatoes, potatoes, all spices (but the cilantro), ½ tsp. jalapenos and beef stock.
3) Simmer over low heat until beef and potatoes are tender.

Serving:
1) Place the finished stew in a soup bowl and top with remaining jalapenos and cilantro.

Lunch Alternate: Southwestern Turkey Stew with Jalapeno Chilis
1) Omit the beef and replace with fresh turkey meat.
2) Omit the beef broth and replace with turkey broth.

Nutrition Facts	
1 Serving	
Amount Per Serving	
Calories	301.0
Total Fat	14.1 g
Saturated Fat	2.9 g
Polyunsaturated Fat	1.1 g
Monounsaturated Fat	8.5 g
Cholesterol	64.6 mg
Sodium	459.6 mg
Potassium	893.2 mg
Total Carbohydrate	14.2 g
Dietary Fiber	2.6 g
Sugars	0.8 g
Protein	29.2 g
Vitamin A	10.0 %
Vitamin B-12	55.1 %
Vitamin B-6	44.3 %
Vitamin C	38.0 %
Vitamin D	0.0 %
Vitamin E	8.1 %
Calcium	3.0 %
Copper	11.3 %
Folate	10.5 %
Iron	18.8 %
Magnesium	13.3 %
Manganese	13.2 %
Niacin	34.5 %
Pantothenic Acid	7.8 %
Phosphorus	32.0 %
Riboflavin	17.5 %
Selenium	36.1 %
Thiamin	14.8 %
Zinc	23.7 %

Day 11

Snack

Fresh Melon Bowl with Minted Syrup and Vanilla-Pistachio Yogurt

Yield: 1 Serving

30% Protein:	4 oz. Vanilla Yogurt
40% Carbohydrate:	½ cp. Cantaloupe Melon (Cubed/Drained)
	½ cp. Honey Melon (Cubed/Drained)
	¼ tsp. Fresh Mint
	1 tb. Honey
30% Fat:	1 tb. Crushed Pistachio Nuts

Method:
1) Combine both melons in a strainer and drain juices.
2) Add honey and mint to the drained juices to make syrup.

Serving:
1) Place the melon in a bowl and top with the yogurt, spoon on the minted syrup and pistachios, garnish with mint sprig

Snack Alternate: Fresh Melon Bowl with Vanilla Yogurt
1) Omit the nuts.
2) Omit the syrup.

Nutrition Facts	
1 Serving	
Amount Per Serving	
Calories	216.8
Total Fat	6.7 g
Saturated Fat	1.8 g
Polyunsaturated Fat	1.6 g
Monounsaturated Fat	3.0 g
Cholesterol	7.4 mg
Sodium	118.0 mg
Potassium	803.5 mg
Total Carbohydrate	32.0 g
Dietary Fiber	2.5 g
Sugars	28.2 g
Protein	9.5 g
Vitamin A	4.2 %
Vitamin B-12	11.4 %
Vitamin B-6	19.9 %
Vitamin C	55.7 %
Vitamin D	0.0 %
Vitamin E	4.0 %
Calcium	24.7 %
Copper	10.0 %
Folate	13.2 %
Iron	4.8 %
Magnesium	12.9 %
Manganese	9.3 %
Niacin	5.1 %
Pantothenic Acid	10.6 %
Phosphorus	24.8 %
Riboflavin	17.8 %
Selenium	8.7 %
Thiamin	14.3 %
Zinc	10.0 %

Day 11

Dinner

Pan Seared Sea Scallops with Rainbow Swiss Chard and Parmesan Gratin

Yield: 1 Serving

30% Protein:	6 ea. Sea Scallops (10/20 size)
	1 tb. Grated Parmesan Cheese
40% Carbohydrate:	2 cps. Swiss chard (chopped)
	¼ cp. GS Apple (diced)
	2 tsp. Seasoned Breadcrumbs (Toasted)
	2 ea. Garlic Cloves (minced)
	1 ea. Sm. Onion (minced)
	1 ea. Md. Tomato (diced)
30% Fat:	2 tsp. Olive Oil

Method:

1) In a nonstick (Teflon) pan, over high heat, sear each scallop until golden brown on both sides. Remove and reserve, with the liquid that weeps from the scallops.
2) Clean the pan and sauté in 1 tsp. of olive oil a minced clove of garlic, then add the breadcrumbs and toast. Transfer to a bowl and add the parmesan cheese, reserve.
3) In a sauté pan (large enough to accommodate) add remaining oil and sauté in order the remaining clove of garlic, onion, tomato, apple, and Swiss chard. Add the scallop juices and continue to simmer over low heat until all liquids reduce.

Serving: Plate by placing scallops on a bed of Swiss chard and topping with the Parmesan breadcrumbs.

Dinner Alternate: Replace Sea scallops with 4oz. grilled chicken breast

Nutrition Facts	
1 Serving	
Amount Per Serving	
Calories	438.5
Total Fat	13.3 g
Saturated Fat	2.0 g
Polyunsaturated Fat	3.7 g
Monounsaturated Fat	6.1 g
Cholesterol	60.2 mg
Sodium	1,250.8 mg
Potassium	2,801.7 mg
Total Carbohydrate	43.0 g
Dietary Fiber	10.9 g
Sugars	4.7 g
Protein	40.8 g
Vitamin A	439.7 %
Vitamin B-12	44.6 %
Vitamin B-6	38.1 %
Vitamin C	136.4 %
Vitamin D	0.0 %
Vitamin E	53.1 %
Calcium	36.3 %
Copper	40.3 %
Folate	24.9 %
Iron	53.8 %
Magnesium	105.3 %
Manganese	84.2 %
Niacin	23.2 %
Pantothenic Acid	11.9 %
Phosphorus	59.8 %
Riboflavin	31.8 %
Selenium	66.9 %
Thiamin	23.7 %
Zinc	22.4 %

Day 11

Snack (Dessert)

Plum and Cherry Streusel Bar

Yield: 1 Serving

30% Protein:	1 tb. Protein Powder (Soy Isolate)
40% Carbohydrate:	¼ cp. Graham Cracker Crumbs
	1 tb. Soy Flour
	2 tb. Rolled Oats (Ground)
	1 tb. Brown Sugar
	¼ cp. Fruit Preserves (Cherry/Plums Combo)
30% Fat:	1 tb. Soy Butter or Unsalted/Sweet Butter

Method:
1) Combine all dry ingredients in a mixing bowl with the soy butter, reserving the fruit preserves.
2) Press half of the streusel into bottom of a three-inch bakeable tin or ceramic ramekin and bake at 275 degrees for twenty minutes.
3) Top with the fruit preserves and cover with more streusel. Bake until preserves bubble and top is browned.

Serving:
1 As is.

Snack Alternate: Raspberry Streusel Fruit Bar
1) Omit the cherry/plum preserves and replace with raspberry.

Nutrition Facts	
1 Serving	
Amount Per Serving	
Calories	165.7
Total Fat	7.2 g
Saturated Fat	2.2 g
Polyunsaturated Fat	2.4 g
Monounsaturated Fat	2.3 g
Cholesterol	0.0 mg
Sodium	84.0 mg
Potassium	109.4 mg
Total Carbohydrate	23.1 g
Dietary Fiber	0.9 g
Sugars	14.0 g
Protein	3.4 g
Vitamin A	1.3 %
Vitamin B-12	5.3 %
Vitamin B-6	4.8 %
Vitamin C	4.3 %
Vitamin D	0.0 %
Vitamin E	0.2 %
Calcium	1.6 %
Copper	8.5 %
Folate	5.1 %
Iron	5.4 %
Magnesium	3.0 %
Manganese	12.1 %
Niacin	6.1 %
Pantothenic Acid	3.6 %
Phosphorus	5.5 %
Riboflavin	3.1 %
Selenium	0.9 %
Thiamin	7.9 %
Zinc	14.1 %

Day 11

Orange Ricotta Protein Pancakes with Mandarin
Honey Syrup

Mandarin oranges are excellent sources of vitamins A and C. Mandarin oranges are easily damaged by cold weather and are in their prime in the late fall or winter. Asia. Canned mandarin oranges are usually of the Satsuma variety. They are scalded in hot water to remove the skin, and then dipped in a solution containing lye to further eliminate any undesirable parts of the fruit, leaving the orange segments. They are then rinsed numerous times.

Carb: Pancakes, Orange, Honey
Protein: Ricotta, Soy Milk, Egg Whites
Fat: Olive Oil

Pan Seared Sea Scallops with Swiss chard and Parmesan Gratin

Gratin is a dish that is topped with cheese or bread crumbs and baked until browned. *Searing* is to brown food quickly over high heat, usually done as a preparatory step for combination cooking methods. *Swiss chard* belongs to the beet family and has crinkly dark green leaves and silvery, celery like. The leaves are prepared like spinach and have a similar tart flavor and the stalks are prepared like asparagus and have a tart, somewhat bitter flavor.

Carb: Swiss chard, Bread Crumbs, Onion, Tomatoes
Protein: Scallops
Fat: Parmesan Cheese, Olive Oil

Southwestern Beef Stew with Jalapeno Chili

Beef is chockfull of nutrients. In order to get the equivalent amount of nutrients as a 3 oz serving of beef, you would have to eat: 11 2/3 (3 oz) servings of tuna for zinc, 7 (3 oz) skinless chicken breasts for B12, and 3 cups of raw spinach for iron!

Carb: Potato, Onion, Tomato, Garlic
Protein: Chicken
Fat: Olive Oil

DAY 11
Ingredient List

<u>Dairy/Eggs</u>
4 oz. Skim Ricotta
1 oz. Skim Milk
1 oz. Egg Substitute
1 oz. Grated Parmesan Cheese
4 oz. Plain Yogurt
1 oz. Soy Butter or Unsalted/Sweet Butter

<u>Dry Goods:</u>
½ oz. ea. Soy Protein Powder, Flour
2 oz. Graham Cracker Crumbs
1 oz. Rolled Oats
½ oz. Brown Sugar
2 oz. Raspberry Fruit Preserves
½ oz. Pistachio Nuts
1 oz. Honey
4 oz. Canned Plum Tomatoes
¼ oz. Cumin, Chili Powder, Coriander
2 oz. Beef Broth
1oz. Olive, Canola Oil
½ oz. Seasoned Breadcrumbs
2 oz. Buttermilk Pancake Mix
2oz. Mandarin Orange Segments
¼ oz. Orange Extract
½ oz. Granulated Sugar (Fructose Preferred)

<u>Meats/Seafood:</u>
6 oz. Sea Scallops
4 oz. Beef Stew Meat

<u>Produce:</u>
1 ea. Orange, Granny Smith Apple
1 ea. Sp. Onion, Tomato
4 ea. Garlic Cloves
1 ea. Sprig Fresh Cilantro, Mint
3 ea. Red Bliss Potatoes
½ ea. Cantaloupe, Honeydew Melon

Day 12

Breakfast

Non-Fat Sour Cream and Raisin Crepes

Yield: 1 Serving

30% Protein:	6 oz. Non-Fat Sour Cream

40% Carbohydrate: 2 ea. Fz. Crepe Shells
 1 tb. Golden Raisins
 1tb. Dark Raisins
 ½ tsp. Granulated Sugar (Fructose Preferred)
 1tb. Cornstarch Slurry (Water +Cornstarch)
 ¼ tsp. Powdered Cloves

30% Fat: 1 tb. Walnuts (Minced)

Method:
1) In a sauce pot macerate (soak) raisins in hot water and sugar. Remove when plump. Reserve.
2) Bring the sugared liquid to a boil and add cloves, then slurry to thicken reserve and cool.
3) Combine the walnuts with the sour cream. Reserve.

Serving:
1) Fill each crepe shell with half of the sour cream and walnut mixture.
2) Place on a plate and cover crepes with raisins and spoon on the syrup.

Breakfast Alternate: Skim Ricotta Cheese and Raisin Crepes
1) Omit sour cream and replace with ricotta.
2) Omit the walnuts.

Nutrition Facts	
1 Serving	
Amount Per Serving	
Calories	414.8
Total Fat	15.1 g
Saturated Fat	2.4 g
Polyunsaturated Fat	7.9 g
Monounsaturated Fat	3.5 g
Cholesterol	93.1 mg
Sodium	381.5 mg
Potassium	568.5 mg
Total Carbohydrate	61.3 g
Dietary Fiber	2.0 g
Sugars	17.7 g
Protein	12.3 g
Vitamin A	8.7 %
Vitamin B-12	8.4 %
Vitamin B-6	9.0 %
Vitamin C	1.9 %
Vitamin D	0.0 %
Vitamin E	3.0 %
Calcium	61.8 %
Copper	16.9 %
Folate	8.3 %
Iron	5.5 %
Magnesium	12.1 %
Manganese	28.5 %
Niacin	3.1 %
Pantothenic Acid	0.9 %
Phosphorus	23.6 %
Riboflavin	17.5 %
Selenium	13.9 %
Thiamin	10.6 %
Zinc	9.0 %

Day 12

Lunch

Ham and Fruit Salad with Honey-Mustard Vinaigrette

Yield: 1 Serving

30% Protein:	4 oz. Deli Ham (Sliced)

40% Carbohydrate:	4 cps. Mesclun Salad Greens
	½ cp. Sliced Peaches
	½ cp. Green Seedless Grapes
	1 tsp. Crushed Mustard
	1 tb. Honey
	2 tb. Cider Vinegar

30% Fat:	2 tsp. Canola Oil

Method:
1) Combine the honey, mustard, cider vinegar, and oil to make vinaigrette.

Serving:
1) Place the greens in a bowl and top with ham and fruit.
2) Pour the dressing over the salad and toss.

Lunch Alternate: Turkey and Fruit Salad with Honey-Mustard Vinaigrette
1) Omit the ham and replace with 4 oz. sliced deli turkey.

Day 12

Snack

Roasted Beets with Creamy Chevre Cheese and Cran-Raisins

Yield: 1 Serving

30% Protein:	¼ cp. Chevre Cheese (Crumbled)
40% Carbohydrate:	¼ cp. Golden Beets (Sliced)
	½ tsp. Cranraisins
	1 cp. Mesclun Salad Lettuce
	1 tsp. Lemon Juice
30% Fat:	1 tsp. Canola Oil

Method:
1) Peel then roast the beets in the olive oil and slice when cooled.

Serving: Place the roasted beets on the butter lettuce, top with the cheese. and garnish with the raisins, drizzle lemon juice.

Snack Alternate: Vine-ripened Heirloom Tomatoes with Maytag Blue Cheese Dressing

1) Omit Chevre cheese and replace with blue cheese.
2) Omit the beets and replace with ½ cp. sliced tomatoes.
3) Combine lemon juice and oil for drizzle.
4) Omit raisins and replace with ¼ cp. hearts of palm.

Nutrition Facts	
1 Serving	
Amount Per Serving	
Calories	210.8
Total Fat	13.5 g
Saturated Fat	6.8 g
Polyunsaturated Fat	0.6 g
Monounsaturated Fat	5.4 g
Cholesterol	19.6 mg
Sodium	307.2 mg
Potassium	136.5 mg
Total Carbohydrate	14.8 g
Dietary Fiber	2.1 g
Sugars	3.9 g
Protein	8.5 g
Vitamin A	14.1 %
Vitamin B-12	1.3 %
Vitamin B-6	7.2 %
Vitamin C	13.9 %
Vitamin D	0.0 %
Vitamin E	4.0 %
Calcium	7.0 %
Copper	19.2 %
Folate	8.8 %
Iron	6.5 %
Magnesium	4.1 %
Manganese	11.6 %
Niacin	1.9 %
Pantothenic Acid	3.9 %
Phosphorus	12.4 %
Riboflavin	11.8 %
Selenium	2.6 %
Thiamin	3.2 %
Zinc	3.8 %

Day 12

Dinner

Roasted Turkey with Acorn Squash Braised in Ginger-Orange Sauce

Yield: 1 Serving

30% Protein:	5 oz. Turkey Breast Cutlet
40% Carbohydrate:	1 cp. Acorn Squash (Peeled/Diced)
	½ cp. Orange Juice
	2 tsp. Brown sugar
	½ tsp. Ground Ginger
	2 tb. Cornstarch Slurry (Water + Cornstarch)
	1 tb. Scallion (Chopped)
30% Fat:	2 tsp. Canola Oil

Method:
1) Place the squash in a braising pan. Sprinkle with brown sugar and orange juice.
2) Place the raw turkey over the squash. Cover and braise at 425 degrees until squash is tender and turkey done.
3) Pour juices into a sauce pan and thicken with cornstarch slurry to form a sauce.

Serving:
1) Place turkey and squash on a plate and spoon sauce over, top with scallions.

Dinner Alternate: Chicken and Acorn Squash Braised in Ginger-Orange Sauce
1) Omit turkey and replace with chicken breast.

Nutrition Facts	
1 Serving	
Amount Per Serving	
Calories	356.9
Total Fat	11.4 g
Saturated Fat	1.2 g
Polyunsaturated Fat	3.2 g
Monounsaturated Fat	6.0 g
Cholesterol	48.8 mg
Sodium	1,163.7 mg
Potassium	1,182.0 mg
Total Carbohydrate	46.8 g
Dietary Fiber	6.8 g
Sugars	23.0 g
Protein	22.2 g
Vitamin A	289.7 %
Vitamin B-12	38.2 %
Vitamin B-6	36.5 %
Vitamin C	130.6 %
Vitamin D	0.0 %
Vitamin E	11.1 %
Calcium	11.2 %
Copper	13.0 %
Folate	16.4 %
Iron	17.7 %
Magnesium	24.4 %
Manganese	20.9 %
Niacin	12.3 %
Pantothenic Acid	16.5 %
Phosphorus	33.0 %
Riboflavin	24.9 %
Selenium	51.8 %
Thiamin	28.9 %
Zinc	10.7 %

Day 12

Snack (Dessert)

Banana and Walnut Cupcake

Yield: 1 Serving

30% Protein: 2 tb. Egg Substitute
                   2 tb. Buttermilk
                   1 tb. Soy Protein Powder

40% Carbohydrate: ¼ cp. Whole Grain Flour
                   1 tb. Soy Flour
                   Pinch Baking Powder
                   2 tsp. Brown Sugar
                   1 ea. Sm. Sugar Peeled Banana
                   ¼ tsp. Vanilla Extract

30% Fat: 1 tsp. Chopped Walnuts
                   1 tsp. Canola Oil

Method:
1) Whisk together the oil and eggs until foamy.
2) Whisk in the sweeteners.
3) Beat in the bananas and then add the extract.
4) Mix in the dry ingredients and walnuts.
5) Pour into cupcake liners and bake in a muffin tin at 300 degrees until cupcake is set

Serving:
1) As is.

Snack Alternate: Banana Cupcake
1) Omit the walnuts.

Nutrition Facts	
1 Serving	
Amount Per Serving	
Calories	148.0
Total Fat	8.9 g
Saturated Fat	0.8 g
Polyunsaturated Fat	4.1 g
Monounsaturated Fat	3.5 g
Cholesterol	0.8 mg
Sodium	108.7 mg
Potassium	227.0 mg
Total Carbohydrate	10.4 g
Dietary Fiber	0.6 g
Sugars	5.8 g
Protein	7.9 g
Vitamin A	5.1 %
Vitamin B-12	13.4 %
Vitamin B-6	11.1 %
Vitamin C	1.1 %
Vitamin D	1.9 %
Vitamin E	6.7 %
Calcium	8.1 %
Copper	14.4 %
Folate	9.5 %
Iron	9.5 %
Magnesium	4.4 %
Manganese	12.0 %
Niacin	11.8 %
Pantothenic Acid	7.9 %
Phosphorus	11.4 %
Riboflavin	16.6 %
Selenium	7.2 %
Thiamin	15.3 %
Zinc	24.4 %

Day 12

Non-Fat Sour Cream and Raisin Crepes

Crepe is a thin, delicate, unleavened griddle cake made with a very thin egg batter cooked in a very hot sauté pan.

Carb: Crepe Shells, Raisins
Protein: Dairy
Fat: Walnuts

Roast Turkey with Acorn Squash Braised in Ginger-Orange Sauce

Acorn squash is a small to medium-sized acorn-shaped winter squash. It has an orange-streaked dark green fluted shell (orange, yellow and creamy white varieties are also available), a pale orange flesh, a large seed cavity and a slightly sweet, nutty flavor.

Carb: Squash, Scallion, Breadcrumbs
Protein: Turkey, Egg
Fat: Olive Oil

Ham and Fruit Salad with Honey-Mustard Vinaigrette

Prepared **mustard** is a mixture of crushed mustard seeds, vinegar or wine and salt or spices. It can be flavored in many ways, with herbs, onions, peppers and even citrus zest.

Carb: Mixed Greens, Fruit
Protein: Ham
Fat: Canola Oil

DAY 12

Ingredient List

Dairy/Eggs:
6 oz. Non-Fat Sour Cream
1 oz. Egg Substitute
1 oz. Buttermilk
2 oz. Chevre Goat Cheese

Dry Goods:
2 ea. Fz. Crepes
½ oz. ea. Dark, Golden Raisins, Cranraisins
½ oz. Cornstarch
1oz. ea. Granulated Fructose, Brown Sugar
1oz. Walnuts
¼ oz. Powdered Cloves, Ginger
1oz. Canola Oil
1oz. Cider Vinegar
½ oz. Honey
¼ oz. Crushed Mustard
½ oz. ea. Soy Flour, Protein Powder
¼ oz. Vanilla Extract
¼ oz. Baking Powder

Meats:
5 oz. Turkey Cutlet
4 oz. Deli Ham

Produce:
1 ea. Sm. Acorn Squash
1 ea. Rib Scallions
1 ea. Orange, Lemon
1 sm. Bag Mesclun Salad Greens
4 oz. Seedless Grapes
1 ea. Peach
1 ea. Sugar Banana
2 ea. Beets (Red or Golden)

Day 13

Breakfast

Crustless Southwestern Quiche with Berry Bowl

Yield: 1 Serving

30% Protein:	4 oz. Liquid Egg Substitute
	½ oz. Monterey Jack Cheese (shredded)
40% Carbohydrate:	¼ cp. Red Onion (diced)
	1 cp. Fresh Spinach (chopped)
	¼ tsp. Garlic Cloves (minced)
	¼ tsp. Jalapeno Peppers (minced) (optional)
	½ tsp. Prepared Dijon Mustard
	¼ cp. Red Peppers (diced)
	2 tb. Yellow Cornmeal
	8 oz. Assorted Fresh Berries
30% Fat:	2 tsp. Olive Oil

Method:
1) In a skillet sauté the onion, garlic, jalapeno, spinach, and red peppers in the oil.
2) Coat the bottom of a bake-able tin or ceramic ramekin (Dish), with release spray (Spam), sprinkle with cornmeal.
3) Place the cooked vegetables on top and pour egg in with the mustard.
4) Top with the cheese and bake at 350 degrees.

Serving:
1) As is.
2) Serve berries on side.

Nutrition Facts

1 Serving
Amount Per Serving

Calories	293.3
Total Fat	11.3 g
Saturated Fat	1.9 g
Polyunsaturated Fat	1.4 g
Monounsaturated Fat	7.1 g
Cholesterol	4.1 mg
Sodium	486.5 mg
Potassium	1,613.9 mg
Total Carbohydrate	29.6 g
Dietary Fiber	9.7 g
Sugars	11.5 g
Protein	21.5 g
Vitamin A	411.1 %
Vitamin B-12	36.1 %
Vitamin B-6	42.3 %
Vitamin C	262.0 %
Vitamin D	17.5 %
Vitamin E	25.9 %
Calcium	39.4 %
Copper	22.9 %
Folate	105.3 %
Iron	61.9 %
Magnesium	48.3 %
Manganese	113.1 %
Niacin	11.5 %
Pantothenic Acid	28.4 %
Phosphorus	36.0 %
Riboflavin	125.6 %
Selenium	47.9 %
Thiamin	36.0 %
Zinc	20.6 %

Day 13

Lunch

Sesame Crusted Fresh Tuna Fillet Salad with Ginger-Citrus Vinaigrette

Yield: 1 Serving

30% Protein:	6 oz. Yellow Fin Tuna Steak

40% Carbohydrate:	3 cps. Mixed Salad Greens
	2 tb. "Lite" Soy Sauce
	¼ cp. Orange Juice
	¼ tsp. Ginger Powder
	¼ tsp. Garlic Powder
	2 tb. Rice Wine Vinegar
	¼ cp. Red Pepper (Slivered)
	¼ cp. Scallions (Slivered)
	¼ cp. Enoki Mushrooms

30% Fat:	1 tsp. Sesame seeds
	1 tsp. Sesame Oil
	1 tsp. Olive Oil

Method:
1) Combine soy sauce, orange juice, ginger, and garlic powders with rice wine vinegar and 1tsp. combined oils to make vinaigrette.
2) Dredge the tuna in half the oil and press sesame seeds onto to both sides.
3) In a pan, sauté the sesame tuna in remaining oils until golden on both sides.

Serving:
1) Combine greens and place finished tuna on bed, top with peppers, scallions, and mushrooms.
2) Pour the vinaigrette over the salad.

Lunch Alternate: Grilled Chicken Salad with Ginger-Citrus Vinaigrette
1) Omit tuna and replace with 4 oz. chicken breast.
2) Omit sesame seeds and oil.

Nutrition Facts	
1 Serving	
Amount Per Serving	
Calories	418.6
Total Fat	12.9 g
Saturated Fat	2.0 g
Polyunsaturated Fat	3.7 g
Monounsaturated Fat	6.0 g
Cholesterol	98.6 mg
Sodium	106.8 mg
Potassium	1,348.9 mg
Total Carbohydrate	20.8 g
Dietary Fiber	3.9 g
Sugars	15.3 g
Protein	55.3 g
Vitamin A	134.4 %
Vitamin B-12	17.1 %
Vitamin B-6	98.9 %
Vitamin C	157.0 %
Vitamin D	3.3 %
Vitamin E	8.2 %
Calcium	13.5 %
Copper	19.9 %
Folate	10.5 %
Iron	25.7 %
Magnesium	37.5 %
Manganese	17.4 %
Niacin	109.1 %
Pantothenic Acid	20.7 %
Phosphorus	48.4 %
Riboflavin	14.6 %
Selenium	116.6 %
Thiamin	66.4 %
Zinc	11.4 %

Day 13

Snack

Roasted Root Vegetable and Ham Croquettes with Herbed Béchamel

Yield: 1 Serving

30% Protein:	¼ cp. Deli Ham (finely chopped)
	½ oz. Egg Substitute

40% Carbohydrate:	2 tb. Seasoned Breadcrumbs
	¼ cp. Chopped Sp. Onions
	¼ cp. Yellow Turnips (diced)
	¼ cp. Chicken Broth
	1 tsp. Fresh Parsley (minced)
	1 tb. Cornstarch Slurry (Water + Cornstarch)

30% Fat:	¼ cp. Non-Fat Half and Half

Method:
1) Combine the half and half and parsley with the cornstarch slurry and thicken over high heat, reserve and cool.
2) Braise the onion and turnips in a separate sauce pot in the chicken broth until tender.
3) Puree all ingredients adding 2 tb. of the cooled sauce (Béchamel).
4) Add the ham and form into a croquettes, dredge in the egg and then the breadcrumbs.
5) Bake at 350 degrees until cooked throughout and golden brown.

Serving:
1) Place the croquette on a plate and pour sauce over.

Snack Alternate: Roasted Root Vegetables and Chicken Croquettes with Herbed Béchamel
1) Omit the ham and replace with ¼ cp. minced turkey.

Nutrition Facts	
1 Serving	
Amount Per Serving	
Calories	211.1
Total Fat	6.4 g
Saturated Fat	2.4 g
Polyunsaturated Fat	0.9 g
Monounsaturated Fat	2.9 g
Cholesterol	37.2 mg
Sodium	1,254.2 mg
Potassium	461.4 mg
Total Carbohydrate	13.4 g
Dietary Fiber	3.4 g
Sugars	6.1 g
Protein	22.3 g
Vitamin A	130.9 %
Vitamin B-12	17.9 %
Vitamin B-6	12.0 %
Vitamin C	8.2 %
Vitamin D	2.5 %
Vitamin E	1.8 %
Calcium	12.4 %
Copper	6.3 %
Folate	5.1 %
Iron	12.7 %
Magnesium	6.0 %
Manganese	4.4 %
Niacin	21.4 %
Pantothenic Acid	9.5 %
Phosphorus	28.8 %
Riboflavin	32.8 %
Selenium	25.1 %
Thiamin	32.5 %
Zinc	14.0 %

Day 13

Dinner

Chicken Tuscany in a White Wine Cream Sauce with Seedless Grapes

Yield: 1 Serving

30% Protein:	4 oz. Chicken Breast (Boneless/Skinless)
40% Carbohydrate:	½ cp. Cooked Lentils (boiled)
	½ cp. Seedless Green Grapes
	5 ea. Spears Asparagus
	2 tb. White Wine
	¼ cp. Chicken Stock
	1 tb. Cornstarch Slurry (Water + Cornstarch)
	¼ tsp. Ground Nutmeg
	¼ tsp. Fresh Tarragon (minced)
30% Fat:	2 tb. Non Fat Half and Half

Method:
1) Combine the wine and stock. Poach the chicken, asparagus, and grapes. Remove and reserve.
2) Thicken stock with slurry. Add half and half, tarragon, and nutmeg to make sauce.

Serving:
1) Place the lentils on a plate with the chicken breast, asparagus, and grapes.
2) Spoon the sauce over the chicken.

Dinner Alternate: Chicken Tuscany in a White Wine Sauce with Seedless Grapes
1) Omit the half and half and replace with 2 tsp. olive oil.

Nutrition Facts	
1 Serving	
Amount Per Serving	
Calories	307.8
Total Fat	2.9 g
Saturated Fat	1.0 g
Polyunsaturated Fat	0.8 g
Monounsaturated Fat	0.7 g
Cholesterol	67.9 mg
Sodium	242.2 mg
Potassium	1,086.8 mg
Total Carbohydrate	40.8 g
Dietary Fiber	10.4 g
Sugars	9.1 g
Protein	38.5 g
Vitamin A	11.8 %
Vitamin B-12	10.8 %
Vitamin B-6	51.1 %
Vitamin C	38.0 %
Vitamin D	0.0 %
Vitamin E	12.5 %
Calcium	8.9 %
Copper	27.5 %
Folate	74.2 %
Iron	28.8 %
Magnesium	23.2 %
Manganese	42.0 %
Niacin	78.5 %
Pantothenic Acid	18.8 %
Phosphorus	52.2 %
Riboflavin	24.4 %
Selenium	38.1 %
Thiamin	30.4 %
Zinc	19.3 %

Day 13

Snack (Dessert)

<u>Raspberry Fruit Cobbler</u>

Yield: 1 Serving

30% Protein:	1 tb. Soy Protein Powder	
	2 tb. Non-Fat Half & Half	
	1 tb. Skim Milk	
	1 tb. Egg Substitute	

40% Carbohydrate:	¼ cp. Whole Grain Flour
	1 tb. Soy Flour
	Pinch Baking Powder
	1 tb. Brown Sugar
	2 tb. Raspberry Preserves

305 Fat:	1 tb. Soy Butter

Method:
1) Combine all ingredients but (fruit preserves) together in mixer and paddle to make cobbler dough.
2) Place Fruit in the bottom of a bake-able 3-inch ceramic ramekin dish.
3) Scoop pastry on top of fruit and flatten.
4) Bake at 325 degrees until fruit is bubbly and pastry is golden brown.

Serving: As is.

Nutrition Facts	
1 Serving	
Amount Per Serving	
Calories	183.2
Total Fat	8.9 g
Saturated Fat	2.8 g
Polyunsaturated Fat	2.9 g
Monounsaturated Fat	2.7 g
Cholesterol	0.9 mg
Sodium	338.2 mg
Potassium	219.5 mg
Total Carbohydrate	19.1 g
Dietary Fiber	0.7 g
Sugars	11.6 g
Protein	7.9 g
Vitamin A	4.2 %
Vitamin B-12	14.5 %
Vitamin B-6	10.8 %
Vitamin C	2.5 %
Vitamin D	1.2 %
Vitamin E	0.6 %
Calcium	15.9 %
Copper	13.7 %
Folate	7.3 %
Iron	10.5 %
Magnesium	3.6 %
Manganese	9.0 %
Niacin	13.9 %
Pantothenic Acid	8.3 %
Phosphorus	14.8 %
Riboflavin	11.8 %
Selenium	6.9 %
Thiamin	14.8 %
Zinc	29.8 %

Day 13

Crustless Southwestern Quiche with Berry Cup

Quiche is a French dish consisting of a pastry crust filled with savory custard made with eggs and cream and garnished with ingredients. *Did you know* that the word "Quiche" is derived from the German word "Kuchen," meaning cake?

Carb: Onion, Spinach, Peppers, Cornmeal, Fruit
Protein: Egg Whites, Jack Cheese
Fat: Olive Oil

Chicken Tuscany in a White Wine Cream Sauce with Seedless Grapes

Grapes are great sources of manganese. Choose grapes that are plump and are on a healthy looking stem. Rinse, loosely wrap in a paper towel, and then keep in a plastic bag in the fridge. Try partially freezing grapes for snacking or add them to your drink instead of ice cubes!

Carb: Lentils, Grapes, Asparagus, Wine,
Protein: Chicken
Fat: Olive Oil

Sesame Crusted Tuna Salad with Ginger-Citrus Vinaigrette

Sesame seeds lend a nutty flavor to foods and they are also a great source of manganese, copper, calcium, and magnesium. If purchasing sesame seeds, make sure there is no presence of moisture, since they can go bad. Hulled seeds should be stored in an air tight container in a dry place. *Ginger* adds a distinguishable, zesty flavor, usually found in Asian cuisines. Ginger is a popular herbal remedy for gastrointestinal relief, preventing motion sickness, as well as other ailments.

Carb: Bok Choy, Peppers, Scallions, Mushrooms
Protein: Tofu
Fat: Sesame Seeds, Sesame Oil, Olive Oil

Roasted Root Vegetable and Ham Croquettes with Herbed Béchamel

Croquette is a food such as ham and potatoes that has been pureed and/or bound with a thick sauce, such as béchamel, then formed into small shapes, breaded, and deep-fried. *Béchamel* is a French leading sauce made by thickening milk with a white roux and adding seasonings.

Carb: Breadcrumbs, Mirepoix, Turnips
Protein: Ham Hock, Egg
Fat: Heavy Cream

DAY 13

Ingredient List

Dairy/Eggs:
5 oz. Egg Substitute
½ oz. Shredded Jack Cheese
4 oz. Non-Fat Half and Half
½ oz. Skim Milk
½ oz. Soy Butter

Dry Goods:
¼ oz. Dijon Mustard
½ oz. Cornmeal
1 oz. Olive Oil
1 oz. White Wine (optional)
¼ oz. Nutmeg, Ginger, Garlic Powder
½ oz. Cornstarch
4 oz. Chicken Broth
2 oz. Dry Lentils
¼ oz. Sesame Seeds
¼ oz. Sesame Seed Oil
1 oz. Lite Soy Sauce
1 oz. Rice Wine Vinegar
1 oz. Seasoned Breadcrumbs
2 oz. Whole Grain Flour
½ oz. ea. Soy Flour, Protein Powder
¼ oz. Baking Powder
½ oz. Brown Sugar
1 oz. Raspberry Preserves

Meats/Seafood:
4 oz. Chicken Breast
2 oz. Deli Ham
6 oz. Yellow Fin Tuna Fillet

Produce:
1 ea. Sm. Red Pepper
1 ea. Sm. Bag Spinach
2 ea. Garlic Cloves
1 pt. Assorted Berries
1 ea. Sm. Red Onion, Scallions, Sp. Onion
1 ea. Sm. Bunch Asparagus
4 oz. Seedless Grapes
1 ea. Sprig Tarragon, Parsley
1 ea. Sm. Bag Mesclun Salad Greens
1 ea. Sm. Bunch Enoki Mushrooms
1 ea. Yellow Turnip or Rutabaga
2 ea. Oranges for Juice

Day 14

Breakfast

"Power" Oatmeal with Nuts and Apple-Cherry Compote

Yield: 1 Serving

30% Protein:	1 tb. Whey Vanilla Protein Powder
	1 cp. Skim Milk
40% Carbohydrate:	¼ cp. Dry Rolled Oats or Irish Groats
	¼ tsp. Powdered Cinnamon
	1 ea. Granny Smith Apple (Diced)
	¼ cp. Frozen Cherries
	½ tsp. Granulated Sugar (Fructose Preferred)
	1 tsp. Honey
30% Fat:	1 tb. Toasted Almond Slivers

Method:
1) In a sauce pot and 1 cp. water combine the apple, cherries, and sugar. Cook until reduced and forms compote.
2) In a separate sauce pot cook the oats in the skim milk adding the honey and cinnamon.
3) Let the oatmeal cool and stir in the protein powder.

Serving:
1) Place the oatmeal in a bowl and garnish with the almonds and the fruit compote.

Breakfast Alternate: Creamy "Power" Oatmeal with Apple-Cherry Compote
1) Omit the nuts and replace with 2 tb. heavy cream.

Nutrition Facts	
1 Serving	
Amount Per Serving	
Calories	492.8
Total Fat	9.0 g
Saturated Fat	1.2 g
Polyunsaturated Fat	2.9 g
Monounsaturated Fat	5.5 g
Cholesterol	10.9 mg
Sodium	413.0 mg
Potassium	788.6 mg
Total Carbohydrate	97.7 g
Dietary Fiber	9.4 g
Sugars	50.4 g
Protein	24.1 g
Vitamin A	21.7 %
Vitamin B-12	5.9 %
Vitamin B-6	11.1 %
Vitamin C	18.7 %
Vitamin D	50.0 %
Vitamin E	21.8 %
Calcium	78.8 %
Copper	24.0 %
Folate	8.1 %
Iron	16.3 %
Magnesium	36.0 %
Manganese	117.8 %
Niacin	6.3 %
Pantothenic Acid	15.6 %
Phosphorus	42.6 %
Riboflavin	31.2 %
Selenium	7.3 %
Thiamin	29.2 %
Zinc	16.0 %

Day 14

Lunch

Turkey Wrap with Herbed Mayonnaise

Yield: 1 Serving

30% Protein:	4 oz. Turkey Breast (Sliced)
40% Carbohydrate:	1 ea. 6" "Low Carb" Wheat Tortilla
	1 ea. Md. Tomato (sliced)
	1 cp. Mesclun Salad Greens
	1 tsp. Mixed Fresh herbs (minced)
30% Fat:	2 tb. "Lite" Mayonnaise

Method:
1) Combine the mayonnaise with the herbs to make dressing.

Serving:
1) Place the tortilla on a plate and top with all ingredients, roll into a wrap.
2) Spoon on the dressing as desired.

Lunch Alternate: Turkey Wrap with Herbed Vinaigrette
1) Omit the mayonnaise and replace with 2 tsp. olive oil and 1 oz. white vinegar.

Nutrition Facts	
1 Serving	
Amount Per Serving	
Calories	334.5
Total Fat	14.6 g
Saturated Fat	2.7 g
Polyunsaturated Fat	0.4 g
Monounsaturated Fat	0.6 g
Cholesterol	59.3 mg
Sodium	1,711.0 mg
Potassium	477.9 mg
Total Carbohydrate	26.8 g
Dietary Fiber	10.6 g
Sugars	7.8 g
Protein	28.2 g
Vitamin A	68.6 %
Vitamin B-12	38.2 %
Vitamin B-6	22.6 %
Vitamin C	39.9 %
Vitamin D	0.0 %
Vitamin E	7.2 %
Calcium	18.4 %
Copper	5.0 %
Folate	3.2 %
Iron	18.4 %
Magnesium	7.2 %
Manganese	3.7 %
Niacin	2.3 %
Pantothenic Acid	8.0 %
Phosphorus	29.0 %
Riboflavin	22.9 %
Selenium	50.2 %
Thiamin	12.0 %
Zinc	8.9 %

Day 14

Snack

Roasted Asparagus with Wisconsin Cheddar Fondue

Yield: 1 Serving

30% Protein:	¼ cp. Shredded Low Fat Cheddar Cheese
	1 tb. Grated parmesan
	2 tb. Non-Fat half and half
40% Carbohydrate:	5 ea. Asparagus Spears
	1 ea. Split Sourdough Roll (toasted)
30% Fat:	1 tsp. Olive Oil

Method:
1) Combine Cheeses with the half and half and simmer over low heat until melted.
2) Roast asparagus in olive oil for twenty minutes in a 350 degree oven until tender and golden.

Serving: Place asparagus on sourdough toast and cover with cheese mixture.

Snack Alternate: Omit toast and replace with ¼ cp. roasted potatoes.

Nutrition Facts	
1 Serving	
Amount Per Serving	
Calories	201.8
Total Fat	10.0 g
Saturated Fat	3.7 g
Polyunsaturated Fat	0.6 g
Monounsaturated Fat	5.2 g
Cholesterol	14.4 mg
Sodium	449.4 mg
Potassium	324.9 mg
Total Carbohydrate	13.1 g
Dietary Fiber	1.8 g
Sugars	1.5 g
Protein	15.6 g
Vitamin A	12.7 %
Vitamin B-12	7.3 %
Vitamin B-6	7.7 %
Vitamin C	18.8 %
Vitamin D	0.0 %
Vitamin E	11.5 %
Calcium	29.2 %
Copper	8.2 %
Folate	28.5 %
Iron	5.9 %
Magnesium	7.3 %
Manganese	11.2 %
Niacin	5.3 %
Pantothenic Acid	3.9 %
Phosphorus	33.9 %
Riboflavin	17.2 %
Selenium	14.7 %
Thiamin	9.5 %
Zinc	10.4 %

Day 14

Dinner

Grilled NY Shell Steak with Roasted Potatoes and Beefsteak Tomatoes, Worcestershire BBQ Sauce

Yield: 1 Serving

30% Protein:	4 oz. Beef Shell Steak (Grass Fed Preferred)
40% Carbohydrates:	½ cp. Red Bliss Potatoes (thinly sliced)
	4 ea. Slices Beefsteak Tomato
	¼ cp. Beef Broth
	1 tb. Worcestershire Sauce
	1 tb. BBQ Sauce
30% Fat:	2 tsp. Olive Oil

Method:
1) Season the steak and grill until desired doneness.
2) Toss potatoes in the olive oil and roast at 350 degrees until potatoes are tender.
3) Make sauce by combining beef broth with BBQ and Worcestershire sauces.

Serving:
1) Place the roasted potatoes on a plate with the grilled steak and layer the tomatoes.
2) Spoon the BBQ sauce on the steak and tomatoes.

Dinner Alternate:
1) Substitute the steak for 4 oz. grilled chicken.

Nutrition Facts	
1 Serving	
Amount Per Serving	
Calories	341.0
Total Fat	14.5 g
Saturated Fat	3.3 g
Polyunsaturated Fat	1.2 g
Monounsaturated Fat	9.0 g
Cholesterol	44.2 mg
Sodium	556.1 mg
Potassium	927.9 mg
Total Carbohydrate	25.3 g
Dietary Fiber	2.1 g
Sugars	6.6 g
Protein	26.7 g
Vitamin A	5.0 %
Vitamin B-12	57.2 %
Vitamin B-6	36.8 %
Vitamin C	35.3 %
Vitamin D	0.0 %
Vitamin E	7.1 %
Calcium	3.8 %
Copper	12.5 %
Folate	7.8 %
Iron	33.1 %
Magnesium	13.2 %
Manganese	8.9 %
Niacin	31.2 %
Pantothenic Acid	7.2 %
Phosphorus	28.8 %
Riboflavin	17.0 %
Selenium	17.4 %
Thiamin	15.0 %
Zinc	29.5 %

Day 14

Snack (Dessert)

<u>Pumpkin Mousse</u>

Yield: 1 Serving

30% Protein: ¼ cp. Low-Fat Cream Cheese

40% Carbohydrate: 2 tb. Pumpkin Puree
                     1 tb. Brown Sugar
                     ¼ tsp. Vanilla Extract

30% Fat: 1 tb. Mascarpone

Method:
1) Whisk together all ingredients in a mixer.

Serving:
1) Spoon into a sundae cup and chill.

Snack Alternate: Banana Mousse
1) Omit the pumpkin puree and replace with banana puree.

Nutrition Facts	
1 serving	
Amount Per Serving	
Calories	108.3
Total Fat	5.4 g
Saturated Fat	2.0 g
Polyunsaturated Fat	1.5 g
Monounsaturated Fat	1.7 g
Cholesterol	4.5 mg
Sodium	389.3 mg
Potassium	129.4 mg
Total Carbohydrate	6.5 g
Dietary Fiber	0.1 g
Sugars	3.0 g
Protein	8.2 g
Vitamin A	23.3 %
Vitamin B-12	5.2 %
Vitamin B-6	1.7 %
Vitamin C	1.0 %
Vitamin D	0.0 %
Vitamin E	0.1 %
Calcium	10.8 %
Copper	2.3 %
Folate	5.5 %
Iron	1.2 %
Magnesium	2.4 %
Manganese	2.4 %
Niacin	0.7 %
Pantothenic Acid	1.4 %
Phosphorus	25.0 %
Riboflavin	6.4 %
Selenium	4.1 %
Thiamin	2.2 %
Zinc	3.5 %

Day 14

Power Oatmeal with Nuts and Apple-Cherry Compote

Compote is a fresh or dried fruit cooked in sugar syrup. *Honey* is a sweet liquid made by bees from flower nectar usually used as a nutritive sweetener. *Did you know that* bees may travel as far as fifty-five thousand miles and visit more than two million flowers to gather enough nectar to produce just a pound of honey?

Carb: Rolled Oats, Apple, Cherries, Honey
Protein: Protein Powder, Skim Milk
Fat: Almonds

Turkey Wrap with Herbed Mayonnaise

Many people use **mayonnaise** for non-culinary uses like hair conditioner, removing stubborn rings, or even removing bumper stickers and their residue! *Did you know* that the **BLT** is the second most popular sandwich in the United States?

Carb: Tortilla, Tomato, Mixed Greens
Protein: Turkey Breast
Fat: Mayonnaise

Roasted Asparagus with Wisconsin Cheddar Fondue

Cheddar cheese is a firm cheese made from whole cow's milk produced principally in Wisconsin, New York, and Vermont. Its color ranges from white to orange and its flavor form mild to very sharp.

Carb: Asparagus, Bread
Fat: Olive Oil
Protein: Cheddar Cheese, Parmesan Cheese, Non Fat Half & Half

Grilled NY Shell Beefsteak and Roasted Tomatoes with Worcestershire Sauce

Worcestershire sauce is a thin, dark brown sauce developed in India for British colonials and first bottled in Worcester, England. *Did you know* the correct pronunciation is WOOS-tuhr-shuhr or WOOS-tuhr-sheer? *Beefsteak tomato* is a large, bright red tomato with a slightly squat, elliptical shape and juicy flesh with many seeds. It is good for eating raw or cooked.

Carb: Potatoes, Beefsteak Tomato, Shallots
Protein: Beef
Fat: Olive Oil

Day 14

Ingredient List

Dairy/Eggs:
8 oz. Skim Milk
2 oz. Shredded Cheddar
½ oz. Grated Parmesan
1 oz. Non-Fat Half and Half
2 oz. Low-Fat Cream Cheese
½ oz. Mascarpone

Dry Goods:
½ oz. Whey Vanilla Protein Powder (Muscle Milk Brand Preferred)
2 oz. Dry Rolled Oats
2 oz. Canned Cherries
¼ oz. Honey
¼ oz. Fructose Sugar
½ oz. Sliced Almonds
¼ oz. Powdered Cinnamon
2 oz. Beef Broth
½ oz. ea. Worcestershire, BBQ Sauce
½ oz. Olive Oil
1 oz. "Lite" Mayonnaise
1 ea. 6" Wheat Tortilla (Low-Carb Preferred)
1 ea. Sour Dough Dinner Roll
1 oz. Canned Pumpkin Puree
½ oz. Brown Sugar
¼ oz. Vanilla Extract

Meats:
4 oz. Beef Shell Steak
4 oz. Deli Turkey Breast

Produce:
1 ea. GS Apple
2 ea. Red Bliss Potatoes
2 ea. Tomato
½ bg. Mesclun Salad Greens
¼ oz. Assorted Fresh Herbs (optional)
5 ea. Asparagus Spears

Footnote

Due to packaging purposes, the amounts for each day's ingredients to be purchased are usually in excess of daily use. I have combined all **seven days** to make a complete list convenient for your one-time shopping experience, yet I am sure that you probably already have some product in your pantry. Please follow along with each day's individual ingredient list. As you prepare your meals, it is wise to check off ingredients from the seven-day shopping list. Or if you wish you may shop accordingly to each daily ingredient list, but do so at least one day in advance.

Some other suggestions are not only to set aside one shopping day, but also to set aside a **baking day** completing all seven days of desserts so as to have your "Dessert Snack" ready to be enjoyed without interruption.

I want you to have fun with this program, become educated in portion control and how to make a better food choice. By sticking with your new diet program, you'll be on your way to better health and noticeable weight loss.

Remember making a better choice in diet and exercise is not only the right choice; it's the only way to a healthy lifestyle. So take your time and read through the recipes and ingredient lists. You're the chef who's preparing healthy and balanced meals for a full week, so enjoy it.

So what are you waiting for? Get cooking!

Days 8-14

Complete Week's Shopping List

NOTE: Check previous week's order list for product overage before repurchasing.

Dairy/Eggs:
1 qt. Skim Milk
½ pt. Non-Fat Half and Half
1 pt. Egg Substitute
½ pt. Skim Ricotta
½ pt. Non-Fat Sour Cream
¼ lb. Soy Butter or Whole Unsalted/Sweet Butter
1 oz. Pepper Jack Cheese
¼ lb. Cheddar Cheese
¼ lb. Low-Fat Cream Cheese
½ pt. Plain Yogurt
¼ lb. Feta or Chevre (Goat Cheese)
½ pt. Buttermilk
1 oz. Mascarpone
1 oz. Grated Parmesan
¼ lb. Skim Mozzarella

Dry Goods:
½ lb. Whole Grain Flour
1 lb. Rolled Oats
½ lb. Soy Flour (Roasted Full Fat Preferred)
¼ lb. Soy Protein Powder (Soy Isolate)
¼ lb. Brown Sugar
¼ lb. Honey
2 oz. Cornmeal
2 oz. Vanilla Whey Protein Powder (Muscle Milk Brand Preferred)
¼ lb. Granulated Sugar (Fructose Preferred)
1 oz. Chocolate Chips (White or Dark)
1 ea. Sm. Bottle Vanilla and Orange Extract
2 oz. Graham Cracker Crumbs
1 oz. ea. (Sm. Box) Dark, Golden and Cranraisins
1 bx. Cornstarch
1 sm. Jar "Lite" Mayonnaise, Crushed Dijon Mustard
½ pt. ea. Olive, Canola Oil

1 ea. Sm. Bottle Sesame Seed Oil
1 pt. ea. Chicken, Beef Broth
1 ea. Sm. Bottle Red Wine, Balsamic, Cider, and Rice Vinegar
1 ea. Sm. Bottle Diet Maple Syrup
1 ea. Sm. Bottle Worcestershire, BBQ Sauce
1 ea. Sm. Bottle Hoisin, "Lite" Soy Sauce
1 ea. Sm. Baking Powder, Soda
1 ea. Sm. Jar Raspberry Preserves
1 ea. Sm. Pkg. Saffron
1 ea. Sm. Can Tomato Paste, Prepared Tomato Sauce
1 ea. 4 oz. Can Italian Plum Tomatoes
1 ea. Sm. Can Pumpkin Puree
1 ea. Sm. Can Cherries, Mandarin Orange Segments
1 ea.4 oz. Can Chick Peas, Black Eyed Peas
1 ea. Sm. Box Buttermilk Pancake Mix
1 ea. Sm. Box Seasoned Bread Crumbs
1 ea. Sm. Box Basmati Rice, Whole Wheat Couscous, Black Chinese Rice, Lentils

Spices:
1 ea. Sm. Jar Powdered Ginger, Cloves
1 ea. Sm. Jar Garlic and Chili, Cumin, and Coriander Powder
1 ea. Sm. Jar Ground Cinnamon, Nutmeg, Black Pepper, Cajun Blackening Spices

Nuts:
1 ea. Sm. Pkg. Hazelnuts, Shelled Pistachios, Sesame Seeds, Sliced Almonds, Walnuts

Breads:
1 ea. 6" Corn Tortilla
1 ea. 6" Whole Wheat Pocket Pita
1 ea. 6" Whole Wheat Tortilla (Low Carb Preferred)
2 ea. 6" Frozen Crepes

1 ea. 6" Sour Dough Dinner Roll

Meats/Seafood:
6 oz. Sea Bass Fillet
6 oz. Sea Scallops
6 oz. Yellow Fin Tuna
3 oz. Salmon Fillet
4 oz. Beef Shell Steak
4 oz. Beef Stew
4 oz. Beef Rib Eye Steak
6 oz. Pork Chop w/Bone
4 oz. Beef Brisket
2 oz. Italian Sweet Sausage
½ lb. Sliced Deli Turkey
½ lb. Sliced Deli Ham
2 ea. 4oz. Chicken Breast Cutlet
4 oz. Turkey Cutlet

Produce:
½ ea. Sm. Butternut Squash
½ ea. Sm. Pineapple
½ ea. Sm. Zucchini
2 ea. Scallion Ribs
1 ea. Sm. Cantaloupes, Honeydew Melon
1 ea. Lg. Carrot
½ pt. ea. Red, Yellow Grape Tomatoes
1 ea. Sm. Japanese Eggplant
2 ea. Granny Smith Apple
3 ea. Sp. Onion
3 lb. Red Bliss Potatoes
1 ea. Sm. Acorn Squash
1 ea. Lemon, Lime
3 ea. Bag Mesclun Salad Greens
½ lb. Seedless Grapes
1 ea. Sugar Banana
2 ea. Beets (Red or Golden)
1 ea. Sm. Red Pepper
1 ea. Sm. Bag Spinach Leaves
1 ea. Bulb Garlic Cloves
1 pt. ea. Blue Berries, Strawberries
3 ea. Sm. Red Onion
1 ea. Sm. Bunch Asparagus
1 ea. Sprig Tarragon, Parsley, Basil
1 ea. Sprig Fresh Cilantro, Mint, Dill

1 ea. Sm. Bunch Enoki Mushrooms
1 ea. Yellow Turnip or Rutabaga
3 ea. Oranges
4 ea. Tomatoes
3ea. Peaches
1 lb. Bok Choy Cabbage
2 oz. Snow Peas
2 ea. Plum Tomatoes

Appendix

Zonies' (40/30/30) Diet
Quantity Guidelines for Entrée Production
(Use Half for Snack)

Proteins: 30%

Red Meats = 4 oz. Cooked Portion.

Beef—180 Choice Shell Strip (Denuded), Pismo Choice Tenderloin Fillet, Choice Top Round, Cubes ¾ Stews, Flank, Fresh Brisket, Corned Brisket, Ground 80/20

Lamb—Choice Top Round, New Zealand Baby Racks (8 Bone), Cubes ¾ Stews, Ground 80/20

Pork—Boneless Loin, Chops, Slab Bacon

Veal—Choice Top Round, Cubes ¾ Stews, Ground 80/20

Poultry (Skinless)—4 oz. Cooked Portion

Chicken, Legs, Thighs/Turkey Breast, Ground

Cheeses (Hard, Semi Soft)—4 oz. Portion

Dairy (Yogurt, Ricotta, Cottage Cheese, Skim Milk)—8 oz. Portion

Eggs (Whites, Substitute, Whole)—4 oz. Cooked Portion

Vegetarian (Tofu Firm, Soft, Silk, Baked, Seitan, Tempeh)—6 oz. Portion

Seafood—6 oz. Cooked Portion

Fatty Fish—Salmon Filets

White Fish—Cod, Scrod, Haddock, Hake, Turbot, Sole, Flounder, Tilapia, Snapper, Barramundi, Bass Filets.

Crustaceans—Pink Shrimp 16/20 P/D, Raw and Cooked, Pulled Blue Claw Crabmeat

Substitutes (Whey/Soy Powders, Gelatin)-½ oz. Portion

Complex Carbohydrates: 40%

Less Dense (Primary): Green, White, Red, Brown, Purple, Yellow Vegetables (Grown Above Ground)—2-3 Volume Cups of Cooked Portion/ Raw Portion-4 Cups

Note: It is impossible to fit this volume into the containers, but please use as close to this as possible

Medium Dense (Secondary)—Root Vegetables, Legumes = ½ Cooked Volume Cup Raw

Dense (Moderately)—Whole Grains (Rice, Oats, Barley, and Wheat) Potatoes, Yams, Corn-½ Cooked Volume Cup

Simple Carbohydrates: Moderate Use

All Processed (Unfavorable)—Breads, Mini Bagel, Corn Bread, Mini Croissant, Biscuit, Dinner Roll, Waffle-1 ea.

Pancakes, Granola, Cereal, Tortilla, Taco, Pita, Chips-½-1 oz. Dry Weight

Sugars (Granulated, Brown)-1 tsp

Condiments (Ketchup, BBQ, Teriyaki Sauce, Diet Syrup)-1 tb.

Fats: 30%

Monounsaturated (Primary) (Olive, Canola, Seed Oils, All Nuts)-1½ tsp.

Polyunsaturated (Secondary) (Soy, Corn, Safflower, Blended Oils, Earth Balance Margarine Spread)-1½ tsp.

Saturated (Moderately) (Butter, Mascarpone, Cream Cheese, Avocado, Tahini, Peanut Butter)-½ tb.

Fruit (All)-1 Volume Cup

U.S. Measurement Equivalents

1 Pinch/Dash = 1/16 teaspoon (tsp)

1 teaspoon = 1/3 tablespoon (tb)

3 teaspoons = 1 tablespoon (tb)

1 tablespoon = 3 teaspoons; 1/2 fluid ounce (oz)

1 shot/Jigger = 3 tablespoons; 1 1/2 fluid ounces (oz)

4 tablespoons = 2 fluid ounces; 1/4 cup (cp)

8 tablespoons = 4 fluid ounces; 1/2 cup (cp)

16 tablespoons = 8 fluid ounces; 1 cup (cp)

1/8 cup = 2 tablespoons; 1 fluid ounce (oz)

1/4 cup = 4tablespoons; 2 fluid ounces (oz)

1/2 cup = 8 tablespoons; 4 fluid ounces (oz)

3/4 cup = 12 tablespoons; 6 fluid ounces (oz)

1 cup = 16 tablespoons; 8 fluid ounces (oz)

2 cups =16 fluid ounces; 1 pint (pt)

4 cups = 32 fluid ounces; 1 quart (qt)

8 cups = 64 fluid ounces; 2 quart (qt)

1 pint = 16 fluid ounces; 2 cup (cp)

2 pint = 32 fluid ounces; 1 quart (qt)

1 quart = 32 fluid ounces; 4 cup; 2 pint (pt)

4 quart = 128 fluid ounces; 16 cup; 8 pint; 1 gallon (gal)

1 gallon = 128 fluid ounces; 4 quart (qt)

8 quart = 1 peck (pc)

'Zonies'
Sparking a Revelation
'Zonies'
'The Written Word'

Can you explain the concept of "burning more calories than you consume" in order to lose weight?

It sounds like you're referring to a "calories in vs. calories out" type of equation. First you need to understand that one pound of fat is made up of roughly 3,500 extra calories. So in order to lose one pound of fat, you need to create a caloric deficit of 3,500 calories.

Basically, you can create a deficit of calories in three different ways:

1) Eat fewer calories than you burn each day. Keep in mind that your body burns calories all day long as part of your basal metabolic rate (BMR), because it takes energy (calories) for your body to perform basic physiological functions that are necessary for life—breathing, digesting, circulating, thinking, and more. On top of that, physical activity (bathing, walking, typing, and exercising) uses even more calories each day.

Example: If you eat 500 fewer calories each day for a week, you'll lose about 1 pound of fat (500 calories x 7 days = 3,500 calories).

2) Burn more calories than you consume by increasing your physical activity. If you eat enough calories to support your BMR, but exercise more, you'll create a caloric deficit simply by burning extra calories. This works only when you're not overeating to begin with.

Example: Regardless of your BMR, if you exercised to burn an extra 500 calories each day, you'll lose about one pound of fat in a week (500 calories x 7 days = 3,500 calories).

3) A combination of eating fewer calories and exercising to burn more calories. This is the most effective way to lose weight and keep it off. It's much easier to create a substantial calorie deficit when you combine dieting with exercise because you don't have to deprive yourself from food, and you don't have to exercise in crazy amounts.

Example: If you cut just 200 calories a day from your diet and burned just 300 calories a day by exercising, you'd lose about 1 pound per week. Compare that to the other examples above—you're losing weight at about the same rate without making major changes to your diet or exercise routine. Some people hate to cut calories while others hate to exercise, so a combination approach allows you to do more of whatever comes easier for you. As long as you are consistent, your calorie deficit will "add up" over time, and you'll slim down.

It's also important to note that although this math seems relatively simple, our bodies are very complicated and you might not always see the results you expect based on equations alone. Many other factors can affect your weight loss rate along the way.

Sparking a Revelation
#1
Overview—Eating Well

The food you eat is the source of energy and nutrition for your body. Eating should be a pleasurable experience, not one that causes guilt or remorse. Getting enough food is rarely a problem, but getting enough good nutrition can be a challenge. What should you eat to stay healthy? Nearly everyone has an opinion, from your best friend to the daily newscaster. There is a lot of advice available, but the basics for good health have not changed since the first fad diets were introduced

Nutrients

Your body needs over forty-five different nutrients every day. These nutrients are essential for health and must be provided in the foods eaten. These nutrients can be divided into five classes:

- <u>Carbohydrates</u> (starches, sugar, and fiber)
- <u>Proteins</u> (includes twenty-two amino acids)
- <u>Fats</u> (saturated, monounsaturated, and polyunsaturated fatty acids)
- <u>Minerals</u>
- <u>Vitamins</u>

These nutrients work together and interact with body chemicals to perform several functions.

- Provide materials to build, repair, and maintain body tissues
- Supply substances that function in the regulation of body processes
- Furnish fuel for energy needed by the body

Each nutrient has a certain special job to do in the building, maintenance, and operation of your body. Some jobs require that nutrients work together as a team. These jobs are nutrient-specific. They cannot be done by other nutrients—an extra supply of one nutrient cannot make up for a shortage of another. <u>That's why a balanced diet</u> including all food groups is so necessary. Your body needs all of these nutrients, not just a few. Some nutrients need to be replenished every day from food while others can be stored in the body as fat for energy use later.

The Energy-Providing Nutrients

Of the six classes of nutrients, only three provide energy: carbohydrates, fats, and proteins. Energy is the body's most basic need. Energy is used when you breathe, when the heart pumps blood, and when you sit, stand, and walk. The more vigorous the activity, the more energy is required.

The energy contained in a carbohydrate, fat, or protein is measured in kilocalories, commonly shortened to "calories" in the United States. <u>The calorie is a measure of energy available to the body</u>. When you eat something, the number of calories it contains is the number of energy units it provides to the body for its needs. The calorie is also a measure of energy your body uses in everyday life or exercise.

Where the Numbers Come From

A bomb calorimeter is a special instrument used to measure calories in food. The food is first dried to remove water and then placed in a special container that rests in water. When the food is burned, heat is transferred to the water. The amount the burning food heats the water is the measure of calories. One calorie is the energy needed to raise the temperature of 1 gram of water 1 degree centigrade.

The energy values of the three calorie-providing nutrients are as follows:

- 1 gram of carbohydrate = 4 calories
- 1 gram of protein = 4 calories
- 1 gram of fat = 9 calories

Calories may also be added to food intake by consuming alcoholic beverages. Alcohol is not a nutrient because it cannot be used in the body to promote growth, maintenance, or repair. It is a toxin that is broken down as an energy (calorie) source and can be converted to fat.

1 gram of alcohol = 7 calories

Nearly all foods supply energy or calories. However, some provide more calories than others. No single food or kind of food is "fattening" by itself. When the energy provided in food is not used—whatever food it is—the excess is stored in the body in the form of fat. Storage of too many excess calories results in being overweight.

Sparking a Revelation
#2
Prime Your Metabolism

Metabolism is the rate at which your body burns its way through calories to keep your heart beating, your lungs breathing, your blood pumping, and your mind fantasizing about Hawaii while crunching accounting figures. Your body is burning calories all the time, even while you're reading this sentence. The average woman burns about 10 calories per pound of body weight every day; the average man, 11 per pound. But that number can vary wildly, and the key to managing your weight over the long haul is to maximize that calorie burn in every way possible.

To that end, you can use the three main types of calorie burn that happen throughout your day. Understand how they work and you'll begin to see how the right foods and a little exercise can turn your body into a full-blown fat-burning machine.

Calorie Burn #1:
The thermal effect of eating

Roughly 10 percent of the calories you burn each day get burned by the act of digesting your food. But not all foods are created equal: Your body uses more calories to digest protein (20 to 35 calories burned for every 100 calories consumed) than it does to digest fats and carbohydrates (5 to 15 calories burned for every 100 calories consumed). That's why adding lean, healthy protein to each meal and snack will help you burn more calories. Even better, protein can dull hunger and protect against obesity, diabetes, and heart disease.

Calorie Burn #2:
Exercise and movement

Lifting weights in the gym, running to catch the bus, twiddling your thumbs during a meeting, and winking at attractive attendees across a crowded room, all fall into this category. It's a common misconception that fit people burn off the majority of their calories at the gym. Even superhero athletes like Tom Brady and Serena Williams only smoke about 10 to 15 percent of their calories by moving their muscles while exercising. That doesn't mean that exercise isn't important, however—it's just not important in the way you think. What exercise really does is to help with Burn #3

Calorie Burn #3:
Basal metabolism

This one's the biggie. Your basal, or resting, metabolism refers to the calories you burn when you're doing nothing at all. Sleeping, watching TV, sitting through yet another mind-numbing presentation on corporate profit-and-loss statements—you're burning calories all the while. In fact, between 60 and 80 percent of your daily calories are burned up just doing nothing. That's because your body is constantly in motion: Your heart is beating, your lungs are breathing, and your cells are dividing, all the time, even when you are asleep.

Sparking a Revelation
#3
The Truth about Sugar

Sugar and High-Fructose Corn Syrup
Simply Avoiding High-Fructose Corn Syrup Won't Save You from Obesity

In the 1970s and 1980s, the average American's body weight increased in tandem with the food industry's use of high-fructose corn syrup (HFCS), a staple because it's cheap.
"Obesity is about consuming too many calories. It just so happens, that a lot of overweight people have been drinking HFCS in sodas and eating foods that are high on the <u>glycemic index</u>—sweet snacks, white bread, and so forth. The calorie totals are huge, and the source just happens to be sugar-based."

The effect of a <u>high-glycemic food</u> can be lessened by adding fat and protein. Spreading peanut butter (protein and fat) on a bagel (starch, which becomes glucose in your body), for example, slows your body's absorption of the sugar.

What matters: We can demonize food manufacturers because they produce foods with enough salt and sugar to make us eat more of it than we should—or even want to. But it comes down to how much we allow down our throats. "A practical guide for anyone is weight." If your weight is under control, then your calorie intake across the board is reasonable. If your weight rises, it's not.

Sugar and Diabetes
Sugar Doesn't Cause Diabetes

Too much sugar does. Diabetes means your body can't clear glucose from your blood. And when glucose isn't processed quickly enough, it destroys tissue. People with type 1 diabetes were born that way—sugar didn't cause their diabetes. But weight gain in children and adults can cause metabolic syndrome, which leads to type 2 diabetes.

"That's what diabetes is all about—being unable to eliminate glucose. The negative effect of eating a lot of sugar is a rise in glucose. A normal pancreas and normal insulin receptors can handle it, clear it out, or store it in some packaged form, like fat."

What matters: That "normal" pancreas? Overeating forces your pancreas to work overtime, cranking out insulin to clear glucose. In today's world, "it's certainly possible that the unprecedented increase in sugar and starch consumption leads to pancreatic burnout." But researchers can't be sure; everyone's body and diet are different, so generalization is iffy. One thing that is sure is that the rise in sugar consumption over the past one hundred years is unprecedented.

Your job: Drop the pounds if you're overweight and watch your sugar intake. Research has shown for years that dropping 5 percent to 7 percent of your body weight can reduce your odds of developing diabetes.

Sugar and Fat
Too Much Sugar Fills Your Blood with Fat

Studies dating back decades show that eating too much fructose, a sugar found naturally in fruit and also added to processed foods, raises blood lipid levels. And while the relatively modest quantities in fruit shouldn't worry you, a University of Minnesota study shows that the large amounts of fructose we take in from processed foods may prove especially nasty: Men on high-fructose diets had 32 percent higher triglycerides than men on high-glucose diets.

Why? Your body can't metabolize a sweet snack as fast as you can eat it. So your liver puts some of the snack's glucose into your blood-stream or stores it for later use. But if your liver's tank is full, it packages the excess as triglycerides. The snack's fructose goes to your liver as well, but instead of being deposited into your bloodstream, it's stored as glycogen. Your liver can store about 90 to 100 grams of glycogen, so it converts the excess to fat (the triglycerides).

What matters: By maintaining a healthy weight, most people can keep their triglycerides at acceptable levels. "If you're overweight or gaining weight, however, they'll accumulate and become a core predictor of heart disease and stroke."

If you're one of those overweight people, your first step is to lay off sugary and starchy foods, beer, and sweet drinks. Your body wasn't built to handle all that sugar. Consider this: You'd have to eat four apples in order to ingest roughly the same amount of fructose in one large McDonald's Coke.

Oral Glucose Tolerance Test
Too Much Sugar Stresses Your System

Doctors use the oral glucose tolerance test (OGTT) to diagnose pre-diabetes and diabetes. For an OGTT, you consume 75 grams of glucose to see how your system processes sugar. It's a kind of stress test—downing that kind of sugar load is not something you should normally do.

And yet a 24-ounce soda often contains *more* than 75 grams of sugar, most of it likely HFCS. Roughly half of that, 75 grams is fructose, so that soda shock may be worse than the doctor's test is. "The way people eat and drink these days, unintentional stress tests probably happen quite often."

What matters: Maybe you figure your body can process a big sugar load without damage. But that's like pointing to a man who smokes until he's ninety and dodges emphysema or cancer. Why gamble?

Severe hyperglycemia (high blood sugar) can cause blurred vision, extreme thirst, and frequent urges to urinate. Hypoglycemia (low blood sugar) is easier to spot: You feel weak with cold sweats and anxiety, blurred vision, or tiredness a couple of hours after a sugar binge. Sound familiar? Ask about an OGTT, which is more accurate than the simpler fasting glucose blood test.

Avoid Blood Sugar Spikes
Fewer Blood Sugar Spikes Help You Live Longer

If you live large—big meals, lots of beer, little moderation—you may be shortening your life even if your weight is okay. Repeated blood sugar spikes stress the organs that make up the metabolic engine of your body. That takes a toll.

And you might not notice. "People can live symptom-free for years in a pre-diabetic state even though they've lost as much as 50 percent of their pancreatic function," says Dr. Lien. "And they don't even know it." People with pre-diabetes share the same health risks, especially for heart disease, that haunt people with full-blown diabetes.

What matters: Moderation? It's simple, yet difficult. Think about what you put in your mouth. Sugar is diabolical; it tastes great *and* is less filling. Back off on the high-impact glycemic: beer, sugary soft drinks and sport drinks, potatoes, pasta, baked goods, pancakes. "The less sugar stress you put on your system, the longer it will function properly."

Sparking a Revelation
#4
7 Habits That Make You Fat

According to recent research, the average person makes two hundred decisions every day that will influence his or her weight. And most of these decisions aren't monumental choices, like "Should I become an elite marathon runner?" or "Should I move to Wisconsin and live entirely on bratwurst and cheese curds?" Most, in fact, are tiny little choices—habits, really—that, over the long run, lead us down one of two paths: the road to ripped or the freeway to flab.

And guess what? That's great news! Because it means that you don't have to run marathons—or even give up bratwurst—to start losing serious weight. You just need to break seven very simple, common habits—tiny changes that have nothing to do with diet and exercise, but have everything to do with dropping pounds, looking great, and making a huge improvement in your health.

Fat Habit #1
Putting the Serving Dishes on the Table

Researchers at Cornell University found that when people served themselves from the kitchen counter or the stove, they ate up to 35 percent less food than they did when the grub was on the kitchen or dining room table. When there's distance between us and our food, the scientists theorize, we think harder about whether we're really hungry for more.

Fat Habit #2
Getting Too Little (or Too Much) Sleep

A sleep schedule is vital to any weight-loss plan, say Wake Forest University researchers who tracked study participants for five years. In the under-40 age group, people who slept five hours or less each night gained nearly 2½ times as much abdominal fat as those who logged six to seven hours; also, those who slept eight hours or longer added nearly twice as much belly fat as the six—to seven-hour group.

People with sleep deficits tend to eat more (and use less energy) because they're tired while those who sleep longer than eight hours a night tend to be less active.

Fat Habit #3
Not Multitasking while Watching TV

We don't need to tell you that too much TV has been linked to weight gain. But here's what you may not realize: You can have your TV and watch it too. Just do something else at the same time. Washing dishes burns 70 calories every thirty minutes. So does ironing. Here's another thing to keep in mind: Cutting TV time even a little helps you burn calories, say researchers at the University of Vermont. In their study, overweight participants who cut their viewing time in half (from an average of 5 hours to 2.5)   burned an extra 119 calories a day. "Nearly anything you do—even reading—uses more energy than watching TV."

Fat Habit #4
Drinking Soda

Researchers say you can measure a person's risk of obesity by measuring his or her soda intake. Versus people who don't drink sweetened sodas, here's what your daily intake means:

½ can = 26 percent increased risk of being overweight or obese

½ to 1 can = 30.4 percent increased risk

1 to 2 cans = 32.8 percent increased risk

More than 2 cans = 47.2 percent increased risk

That's a pretty remarkable set of stats. You don't have to guzzle Double Gulps from 7-Eleven to put yourself at risk—you just need to indulge in one or two cans a day. Wow. And because high-fructose corn syrup is so cheap, food marketers keep making serving sizes bigger (even the "small" at most movie theaters is enough to drown a raccoon). That means we're drinking more than ever and don't even realize it. In the 1950s, the average person drank 11 gallons of soda a year. By the mid-2000s, we were drinking 46 gallons a year. A Center for Science in the Public Interest report contained this shocking sentence: "Carbonated soft drinks are the single biggest source of calories in the American diet."

Fat Habit #5
Taking Big Bites

Dutch researchers recently found that big bites and fast chewing can lead to overeating. In the study, people who chewed large bites of food for three seconds consumed 52 percent more food before feeling full than those who chewed small bites for nine seconds. The reason: Tasting food for a longer period of time (no matter how much of it you bite off) signals your brain to make you feel full sooner, say the scientists.

Fat Habit #6
Not Eating Enough Fat

You don't have to go whole hog on a low-carb diet to see results. Simply swapping a few hundred calories of carbs for a little fat may help you lose weight and reduce your blood-insulin levels, according to researchers from the University of Alabama at Birmingham. People in their study who consumed just 43 percent of their calories from carbohydrates felt fuller after four hours and maintained their blood-sugar levels longer than those who ate 55 percent carbs.

Carbs can cause blood-sugar levels to spike and then crash, leading to hunger and overeating; fat, on the other hand, keeps you satiated longer.

Some easy swaps: butter instead of jam on toast; bacon instead of potatoes; low-fat milk instead of a sports drink.

Fat Habit #7
Not Getting the Best Guidance!

Signing up for e-mails (or tweets) that contain weight-loss advice can help you drop pounds, a new study reveals. When researchers from Canada sent diet and exercise advice to more than a thousand working adults weekly, they discovered that the recipients boosted their physical activity and ate smarter. People who didn't receive the reminders didn't change.

Sparking a Revelation
#5
Weight-Loss Rules You'll Love to Follow

1. **Eat more often.** Out-of-control hunger is a common predictor of overeating—and giving up on any diet. When you go too long without food, your blood sugar drops, your mood and focus plummet, and you often grab the easiest thing you can, which usually isn't healthy. Instead of skipping meals and starving yourself, don't go more than three to four hours without eating. This will keep your hunger monster at bay and keep you happy and satisfied on your program.
2. **Treat yourself.** When you decide that a particular food (or even an entire food group) is off limits for your diet, we focus on that one food even more than if we simply allowed ourselves permission

to eat it from time to time. So give yourself permission—and make a plan—to make room in your diet for your favorite treats.

3. **Stop searching for the best workout.** What's the ideal workout for weight loss? The workout you'll actually do—not the one that worked for your friend or that you heard burned the most calories. Research shows that if you can match the exercise plan to your preference and personality, you'll be more consistent. If you pick what works for others or what you perceive is best despite not enjoying it, you're setting yourself up for failure. When you find something that is fun, care about how many calories it burns.

4. **Love what you eat.** When you eat or drink anything, do so slowly, mindfully, and without distraction. By doing so, you'll increase your enjoyment and slow down your eating, which will allow you the time to notice when you've had enough.

5. **Lie around and do nothing.** Getting seven to eight hours of sleep every night is essential for weight loss. Individuals who are sleep deprived have higher levels of the hunger hormone ghrelin and lower levels of the fullness hormone leptin, which causes them to eat more calories.

6. **Don't skip breakfast.** Think you'll be saving calories by skipping your morning meal? Think again. After an all-night fast, the best way to jump-start your metabolism is to eat within the first hour of waking. Studies have shown individuals who skip breakfast tend to over-consume at lunchtime or later in the day, offsetting all the calories they saved by skipping breakfast.

7. **Dig into carbohydrates!** Lately, carbs have gotten a bad rap. But not all carbs are created equal. We'd all be better off skimping on processed foods and refined flours that make up so many snack foods. There's no reason to give up all carbs, especially the whole sources you'll get in healthful fruits, vegetables, beans, legumes, whole grains, and dairy products.

8. **Go out to eat.** One of the first things people are told when losing weight is to cook more at home and stop eating out. This is good advice in general—but you don't have to give up on a fast takeout meal or your favorite restaurant in order to slim down—especially these days when restaurants are creating healthier, lighter fare than ever before, and sharing those nutrition facts on menu boards and their websites. There are loads of ways to enjoy eating out without blowing your diet. Many menus offer lighter options, and good chefs are more than willing to accommodate special requests.

9. **Indulge in gourmet delights.** If you eat foods you don't enjoy, you'll feel dissatisfied and find yourself searching for more food, even if you aren't hungry. A few more budget-friendly luxuries might be gourmet coffee and tea or a small bar of rich, dark chocolate. Seek pleasure from your foods as much as your budget allows.

10. **Keep your workouts short.** Short bouts, as little as ten minutes at a time, done several times over the course of the day, have similar calorie burning and health benefits as long, sustained sessions. What's more, surveys of the most motivated found that those who exercised less than thirty minutes a day got better weight loss results than those whose exercise plans called for an hour or more a day.

11. **Hang with your friends.** Having support and camaraderie is a huge help while working on healthy lifestyle changes. Make weight loss a team effort by asking friends with similar goals to work out with you. Rather than go out for meals, cook healthy potluck dinners together. Participate in weight loss forums. You can swap healthy recipes, share success stories and disappointments, and have friends to whom you are accountable and who are also there to cheer you on.

12. **Go shopping!** If you love to shop or hunt for bargains, then you'll have fun scoring deals on all the gadgets and gear you need to change your lifestyle. If part of your plan is to cook at home more, shop for the kitchen tools you'll need (think sauté pan, griddle pan, or blender), fun storage containers, plus an insulated bag for your snacks and lunch when you're out for the day.

13. **Don't diet.** This may be the most important rule of all. "Going on a diet" implies a start and a stop, but that's not how sustainable weight loss is achieved. Diets often slow down your metabolism due to the drastic cut back in calories your body is used to, and many diets that are advertised today are just plain unhealthy. Following rigid plans requires constant willpower, something we know humans have only a short supply of! Change and adjust your lifestyle habits a little at a time, and you will lose excess pounds and achieve and maintain the healthy body weight that is right for you. From now on, <u>define the word "diet" as the food plan you use to maintain a healthy body weight</u>, supply you the energy to support your busy lifestyle, and keep you well.

Recommended Reading List

Daust, Joyce and Gene. *40/30/30 Fat Burning Nutrition,* Wharton Publishing, Del Mar, California.

Miller, Powell, Wolever, PhD's. *The Glucose Revolution*, Marlowe & Company, New York.

Sears, Barry, PhD. *A Week in the Zone,* HarperCollins Publishers, New York.

Sears, Barry, PhD. *Zone Food Blocks,* HarperCollins Publishers, New York.

Herbst, Sharon, and Ron *Food Lovers Companion,* Barron's Educational Series, Inc. Hauppauge, New York.

JOURNALS
Sparkspeople.com

#1—Overview—Eating Well
#2—Prime Your Metabolism
#3—The Truth about Sugar
#4—7 Habits That Make You Fat
#5—Weight-Loss Rules You'll Love to Follow